WPB

God Speaks In Dreams:
Connect With Him And Each Other

Carol Oschmann

God Speaks In Dreams:
Connect With Him And Each Other

Carol Oschmann

WE PUBLISH BOOKS
UNITED STATES OF AMERICA

We Publish Books
P.O. Box 1814
Rancho Mirage, CA 92270

www.WePublishBooks.com
E-mail: WePublishBooks@gmail.com

Library of Congress Cataloging in Publication Data:
Library of Congress Control Number: 2005937937

Oschmann, Carol
God Speaks In Dreams: Connect With Him And Each Other

Printed in the United States and London

Photograph by Captain Larry E. VanHoose
Cover designed by Rhonda Clifton Lyons

God Speaks In Dreams: Connect With Him And Each Other / by Carol Oschmann

     SELF-HELP / Dreams SEL012000
     BODY, MIND & SPIRIT / Dreams OCC006000
     RELIGION / Inspirational REL036000

ISBN-13: 978-1-929841-46-2 Hard Cover
ISBN-10: 1-929841-46-9   Hard Cover

ISBN-13: 978-1-929841-45-0 Paperback
ISBN-10: 1-929841-45-5   Paperback

First Printing 2005
Second Printing 2006

We Publish Books

Table Of Contents

Preface *ix*
Introduction *xvi*

Preface

One Aspect of Spiritual Communication

You'll read of ways to increase your awareness of spiritual communication, the gifts this can bring and the richness that can be added to your life. What better place to start than the birth of a child; or to look back at the possibilities missed at your own birth.

Wouldn't it be helpful if we knew, before our children are born, what talents they have and what they should do with their life? We could try and make sure they were exposed to these things while growing up.

This information is available to all parents about to give birth. The soul of the child communicates with us in our dreams. Once the child is born, memories gradually become locked in his or her subconscious. The things we, as parents, teach them, the influence of their teachers, and many other factors, often lead them in opposing directions.

Being loving parents, wanting the best for our children, we look for signs as the child develops their talents and personality. We try to guess where our child excels. We also rely on unexpected opportunities.

Catching clues to a child's purpose on Earth in a few dreams, would eliminate all the time and speculation we now wade through. Recording a mother's, father's, grandparent's, or friend's dreams prior to birth can give your child a head start.

Nine children have allowed me access to information about them before they were born. Generally, the birth date is given in the dream and that proves to be true. If a pregnant woman asks me to dream, either the soul of the baby or a guardian angel comes that night.

As might be expected, a baby is very much concerned about the body it is going into. A young lady named Trish asked for a message from her baby while she was in her fifth month of pregnancy. Since this was the earliest I've dreamed for a child, I found the information about building the body interesting.

This is the dream, which came that night. It compared her earthly body, the one that was building in her mother's womb, to the building of a house. This is one of the universal dream symbols. I stood with the soul of her baby on a hill overseeing a street of earthly homes. He/she is showing me the house that is to be its new body. The house of its body is at the bottom of the hill and still under construction. We go down and into the house to inspect the workmanship. The child is very much interested in the quality of the work being done. The dream ended.

The message I received for Trish was that her baby was concerned about how her mother-to-be was building her earthly body. She wanted Trish to do her part with as much concern. Her mother should follow any good advice she receives, such as eat healthy foods, and stay away from substances known to injure the building of this important body. The mother was smoking.

The houses adjacent to the mother's and her baby's are attached. My guess would be they represent the father and grandparents. The other houses portray the homes of other souls waiting to be in a community with this baby, the relatives, schoolmates, teachers and friends. They were already built and watching the construction.

I wonder what would come from a two-month-old fetus. Would I see more than one soul? Are souls still choosing, shopping around for the best parents? I've come to believe that a soul comes into it's chosen body, fully, near birth. There is another instance where an eight month fetus was also watching the building of its body with a worried eye toward the upcoming due date. However, don't misunderstand. Your baby is near to you. Continue to read, sing, and talk to it. Teach it another language if you can. How about those experiments in sign language? That's a fascinating concept.

Sometimes the soul of a yet–to-be born baby is surprised that I would want to communicate. This type of research is just as unheard of there as it is here. But the soul always warmed to the idea.

In fact, one girl talked to me with the aid of a TV microphone, treating me as though I were a reporter. She showed me a great deal about her future self. She allowed me to tag along behind her as she interacted with others she would know. She showed a great sense of humor by putting notes on people's backs as we passed them on the sidewalk. In the home (of her future?) a man lay on the floor in front of the TV set. She got him off the floor quickly! He was happy to be playing games with her. I realized he was to be her father.

Then she demonstrated her head for business and clothes designing. People, in the dream, came from all over to purchase women's golf shorts she had designed. The attraction to the clothes was either the shorts or the back support that came with them.

It may take twenty years and more to see if this information is true. Her birth date given in the dream was correct and quite different from the date predicted by the doctor.

My first meeting with the baby after birth always leaves me feeling as though I've just met an old friend. The baby's eyes always pop open on hearing my voice. I like the feeling. Of course some people say my imagination is working overtime!

Sometimes in a dream I'm met by a being other than the baby. It may be a guardian angel. Other times, it's a man I've come to call the Keeper of the Gate, the gate being the entryway from that world to this. He is dressed in white robes with pure white hair and beard coming to his knees.

It's difficult to believe that every child dreamed for will accept that this really happened. As the child grows and learns of these dreams, the least and best to be learned by him is that he has a guardian angel. Thinking back, it might have been nice if someone had told me, as a child, that I had a personal angel loving, watching, and helping me!

Some parents have put the typed dreams I gave them in a frame and hung it on their bedroom wall. As the children learn to read, perhaps they may have a closer sense of their own angels.

The first time I had this experience of communicating with the world before birth was when a friend was waiting for her second child. I was uneasy about the impending birth. As I went to bed on January 28, 1988, I said a prayer asking that the birth be swift and easy and the baby healthy. I told God that I couldn't wait to meet this little person.

I began to dream immediately on falling asleep. I saw a huge, old mansion. My feet climbed the steps to the porch. An old man in a long white robe opened the door. A white beard touched his knees, The Keeper of the Gate.

"I was expecting you," he said. Turning, he led me down a hallway and into a bedroom. "We need to remove his suit and prepare him for his life on earth."

There in a huge, old four-poster bed, cobwebs strung from post to post, lay a figure in a space suit. We swept the cobwebs aside and quickly changed his clothes. I wondered about the date he would be born. "February 10", the gatekeeper replied to my thoughts. "He is an old soul and has much to offer the world," he added.

The baby was born two weeks later on February 10. He has proven to be an old soul, indeed. He displays an understanding of people's motives, a self-reliance and has a grasp of ideas way beyond his years. He is special.

I've found that many special souls are coming back now. We need them to help us through the coming years. This next baby may be one of them. The dream suggests that.

As the time for another baby approached, I asked for information on him, when he would be born. On January 3, 1992, one month before he was to be born, he and I met in a dream.

We are in heaven with many angels waiting for a parade. A car came honking and racing from the left. The driver pointed for us to look back. "People are drowning", he shouted. We hurry there.

A large rectangular hole is filled with muddy water. Several people fell in. Some got out.

"Don't stir the waters," I say. "If we focus our eyes we can see through the water to anyone who might be underneath."

"Yes," my new friend yells back. "There's a body! Drag it out!" That is done.

I say, "Let's jump in at the far end. We'll form a chain and walk the pool to make sure we find everyone."

He is beside me all the way. We find no more bodies so we climb out. I kneel down to be his size. He gives me a big hug. "I'm going swimming in that pool in one month," he says.

This is the pool of souls going to be born on earth. There had been a small problem and the water had gotten muddy.

"Shall I keep these clothes on?" he asks.

"It's best to take them off," I reply. "You will need dry clothes when you come out." I wonder if the "clothes" are his power to save people from drowning.

"This feels okay," he says.

"The choices are yours." Someone says. "You will be able to determine your own future. For now you must follow the rules".

This person (his guardian angel?) shows us where to take his clothes. We are in the hospital where he will be born. This, again, tells me the same clothes, his persona, who he was meant to be, are the same in life on earth as they were that day rescuing people in heaven.

I open a door and see a nurse at work. After closing the door we go around a corner and see his parents anticipating his arrival. They see us even though we are still in spirit. They offer to take the boy into their life. They have much joy to share. The dream ended.

I wake up singing. "Go tell it on the mountain."

The boy was born exactly one month later, just as he told me in the dream. The family is Catholic. Later I read that traditional Catholic families, from generations past, hoped one son would be a priest. The boy in my dreams was saving people's souls from the muddy waters of life on earth. Time will tell.

His sister was to be born in early March, 1994. On March 1st I prayed to speak to her in my dreams.

I saw myself entering a house that was still being built. The house represented her body. I looked and looked but had trouble finding her. There she was. Behind a large glass door, like the sliding glass door to a patio, sat a lady surrounded by angels. They were watching the construction from a safe place.

Through the glass I asked, "When?"

"Two weeks," was her reply.

She was born on March 15. She came when she said she would but the house for her soul, her body, was not finished. She nearly bled to death from a hole in her stomach.

We worried as she was rushed to the trauma unit of another hospital where the hole was repaired. Her angels were and are with her. I hope she grows up knowing her angels are just a voice away.

Other mothers have asked for communication with the souls of their unborn babies.

Elaine, the mother of the baby with the TV microphone, had not expected all the details. At 5:30 AM I reminded God that Elaine just wanted to know things like whether the baby would sleep all night, or how to get her to do that. As I fell back to sleep a song went through my mind, over and over.

"Whenever I'm ...whenever I'm away from you. A lullaby will make my dreams come true. I'm just hanging around ... with my head ... up ... upside down ...for you ..." I slipped into the last dream.

Elaine is unloading tons of baby stuff from her car. The baby makes some gurgling noises from the back seat where she is in her seat. They're going to a baby contest. A judge is sitting in his car and is curious about how Elaine will handle the baby. He drives up and their eyes meet across the top of the car. Elaine has large bags of baby stuff piled on the ground all around her. Will she be patient? Will she be short tempered?

This last dream was God's answer to my last question. Raising a baby is not a contest but raising a precious soul.

The song, I took to be from the child. What a sense of humor. She was singing about hanging around, upside down. That was her position in the womb at that time. On a more serious note, she was asking for music.

The date came in the beginning, Nov. 28. This was two months past what the doctor had predicted and she was a rather large baby. This was the date she came.

All dream stories will take 20 years to prove true or false. One thing common to all the babies I contacted were the dates of birth.

My view of truth has changed. You do not have to accept my view of reality. Perhaps your messages will lead you in a different direction. Dream messages are personal. God is leading us to fulfill our part. He is helping us to be the person He prepared us to be. He is helping us to become that piece of humanity's puzzle we were meant to be.

My view of birth, now, is that we choose our parents before we come into this lifetime. Sometimes we choose them for what they can teach us and sometimes for what we can teach them.

If a child dies early and he really needs this mother, I believe he will wait around for a better time. Perhaps the soul will come as a grandchild or a niece or nephew.

If a baby is to be put up for adoption I believe the soul knows ahead of time and also knows the outcome. The child wants to be with a mother who cannot give birth to her own child and must adopt. The child not only chooses the parent but chooses the circumstances as well.

The problems we suffer as children make us stronger people. If a soul needs to suffer certain humilities in order to pass certain of life's lessons and grow, he chooses a parent that will direct him into the necessary scenario.

What lessons does an innocent child have to learn? When I asked the question I received an answer concerning reincarnation and karma. I wonder, do some get caught in that muddy pond and accidentally land with the wrong parents?

Do they need to suffer certain traumas in order to be more effective in their roles as adults? More effective in their roles when back, once again, in heaven? I see Vi's story, beginning in Chapter 1, hinting at this. This may help explain and accept or show you how to adjust to certain things in your life also.

There have been several good books written on the subjects of karma, reincarnation and the soul's purpose and I include some personal choices at the end of this book under the Recommended Reading Section.

If you think I have a special gift, you are wrong. Through my group work and research done by others such as Henry Reed, Ph.D., Robert VandeCastle Ph.D. and others, we now know that this is a natural ability we all share. This is the world God created so we can communicate with Him!

How can you perfect your ability to communicate on the spiritual level? Chapter one is about one lady who came about this knowledge unexpectedly while trying to overcome her constant nightmares and the ways it changed her life.

Enjoy ~ Carol Oschmann

Introduction

I bring to you a true story of an ordinary woman who lived her ordinary life beset by many soul-crushing problems, such as we all meet at times. Unlike most of us, she developed a sure method of seeking and finding solutions to these upheavals -- thru dream interpretation.

I had the privilege of personally knowing the subject of this story, whom we'll call Vi. Vi came from humble, even troubled beginnings. Her parents divorced when she was eight and she chose to live with her father's mother. She became a quiet child, never asserting herself, always obeying for fear of loosing her happy home once more.

Like a lot of us, hers is a story of suppressed yearnings and repressed natural tendencies. To ask her at 20, 30 or even 40 years of age if she felt she had done a good job being herself, she would have said yes. She had a wonderful husband, raised three great children, built and run two businesses (one of them for another person). Her one creative ability was to take a challenge and make the best of it. She had never questioned the meaning of life. She did what she had to do.

She contributed to her family's welfare, often with the mistaken view that her own wants and needs were less important. If they were healthy and happy, she would be the same. Her own needs like proper foods, exercise, talents, and fun came last. In fact, she didn't even know she was missing out on anything.

Nowhere were there clues that she was destined for anything any greater, or worse. She knew she was among the struggling, little people of the world.

It has long has been said we each come into this world with a purpose, a personality, talents and the ability to dream.

Vi found her purpose through her nightly dreams. A lot of American people, bent on making a living and caring for their families, believe that finding meaning in dreams is a phenomenon found only in the Bible or a superstition of some other culture.

Vi had many nightmares. She had many ways of turning them off. Then came a point in her life when the monsters of her dreams seemed to invade every part of her life, her family, her friends, her neighbors, her work, her finances, her health.

Later contemplation had her comparing this time in her life to the Bible's Book of Revelations where the locusts invade every part of the earth. She felt she knew those locusts. They could have been the monsters of her dreams. Her nightmares were key.

The word, revelation, in the Webster's Dictionary, means "something revealed, an act of revealing, especially a dramatic disclosure of something not previously known or realized." This is exactly where this story is headed. The next two years brought many revelations, many good changes.

We'll let Vi tell her own story.

Dedication

To unrealized potential everywhere,
To the spreading of a peaceful energy,
To my Dream Master who led me,
To my first grandson, Kris,
    who showed interest in my writing
    from the beginning,
To my personal rock, who witnessed
    the changes with me, my husband,
To my dream groups and dreamers everywhere,

I dedicate this book,

And send a special thanks to Richard.

Part One

Violet's Story

Once again, in sharing her dreams, Vi was able to give someone a gift.

Chapter 1

Violet's Story
1987

Violet gazed out her new sliding glass door; past the new deck that encircled her home, at the beautiful marina full of grass, sunshine, water, and boats. She started each morning here, thanking God for making her the caretaker of this beautiful property.

The marina radio burped out voices, "Naughty Lady calling Summer Breeze. Naughty Lady calling Summer Breeze." She smiled as she brought her morning coffee to her lips. She enjoyed building stories around these transmissions. Just such a story had landed her first job as a writer. Now, boaters were reading her travel pieces and viewing her photography all across the Great Lakes region. It was bringing in good money, too. And the publisher had just called, telling her to expect a TV producer to contact her about writing for a TV program titled Great Lakes Boating.

"Who'd have believed my life would take this path. No one who knew me at 15, at 25 or even all the way into my forties would have believed stupid, lazy Vi could go so far," she was thinking.

And then there was her new psychic gift.

A small boat came into the harbor from the lake. She recognized Al. Al built the deck and installed the sliding glass door as a gift for saving his life. He'd slipped into that dark pit life sometimes hands us. His business partner (in a restaurant) had disappeared with all his money. How was he to make a living? Vi recalled how she'd taken his question to God one night before going to sleep and how the answers he needed had come in her dreams. Al suddenly had a reason to live, a way to go on making a living and a new belief in God.

Within the last two years she had discovered this ability to get answers from God for other people's problems. Best of all, God seemed to be bringing these people to her. She'd never laid eyes on Al before the day he first boated into the harbor looking for gas. He was staying at his mother's cottage a few miles down the coast. He'd struck up a conversation with Vi's husband, Ray, that led to the three of them having supper together.

Al was clearly asking for a miracle like his aunt had once had in Lourdes. "I'm living off my mother, for crying out loud." He said. "How do I make a living? What's retirement when you've been in business for yourself all your life and now that money's gone too?" He was far too worried to be embarrassed telling these things to total strangers.

Vi told him of her abilities and promised to take his problem to her dreams and see what God had to say. The rest is history, Vi thought. That night as she lay back on her pillow, a vision of Al's essence, something basic to his being, swept through her consciousness. A night of dreams had begun.

Someone pounded on her door, rudely waking her.

After checking the doors to her home, reality finally became clear. No one was there. She should have known it was a dream vision. Her dog would be barking if someone were at the door! She wrote it on the pad of paper she always keeps next to her bed.

As she lay back, fears about Al entered her mind. What did she know about him? At dinner he boasted of his mafia connections - people he'd known in high school. He mentioned names they'd read in the newspaper. Were they just old acquaintances? What, or who, was Vi letting into her mind? Still, God had clearly brought him. God would protect her. She went back to sleep.

Her dreams that night showed Al repairing faucets in an apartment while the residents watched. Next, he was repairing something with wood. All night he went up and down stairs, carrying tools. Then she saw him smiling his way to a bank with full pockets.

Early the next morning, Al was at Vi's door.

"So, that's what I saw in my dreams," Vi related over coffee. She was clearly puzzled as to the meaning. "Does it mean anything to you?"

"Yeah. I trained to be a carpenter, first job out of school." Al was excited now. Over the years, I bought a few apartment houses and then sold them to start the restaurant. I've torn out walls and fixed all kinds of plumbing."

She asked him, "There are multiple dwellings in this area that should be easy to buy. Is that a possibility?"

"Sure is. You got the answer," Al was thinking out loud. "Fixer-uppers are perfect for me. Make the repairs. Collect the rents and who needs to retire? Violet, I'd like to pay you." As he spoke he actually held Vi's hand. "You've helped me more than you can imagine. I have actually been considering suicide. Now I have a reason to go on."

"Having a chance to help is payment enough." Vi replied pulling back.

Al persisted. "How about a sliding glass door, right here, and a deck?"

"Thanks, but I don't think I can afford the lumber right now," she replied.

"I'm a carpenter, remember? That means I've got connections." Al jotted a name and phone number on a piece of paper. "Call this guy. Mention my name and that I need wood for a job. He'll give it to you at wholesale price. Come on. Let's go out and measure up what you'll need."

Once again in sharing her dreams, Vi was able to give someone a gift. Her own reward is the realization that God, the angels, some superior being, offered her the opportunity to solve a problem in another's life. This time she received a bonus! A sliding glass door and a deck!

In the several years since all this happened, I've learned that Al is now a building inspector for the city, which seems just about right, considering what she saw in the dream.

Al was pointed in the right direction. He could make a good living and had new faith that God was watching over his future. Best of all, he no longer entertained thoughts of suicide. God did it, Vi thought. And He used me as the messenger.

Her thoughts drifted to the man in the canoe who'd been lost on the lake last week for three days. Lake Ontario is a big lake, some forty miles wide at that point. That first phone call for help came to the marina. The people lived about two miles west of the marina on the lakeshore. The wife made the frantic call. "My husband's being taken out into the lake by the current. We don't have a boat to get him.

Please help!"

Ray went out on the lake immediately while Vi alerted the coast guard auxiliary who also went out. Vi stayed and coordinated the radio traffic. They spent hours looking for him and could not find him. The lake was picking up, due to a strong storm system over Lake Erie to the west. Those storm systems were moving their way, fast. They'd notified the Canadian Coast Guard, as he seemed to be drifting that way when last seen. They'd notified the American Coast Guard. Helicopters and boats had been out all that afternoon and first night. People had pretty much given up on him by the next morning and Vi organized the local fire departments into shore searches. No body was found.

Vi went to bed and fell asleep. She woke up in the middle of the night knowing exactly where on the lake he was and that he was alive. Her dream had been of traveling down a busy commercial street in the dark of night but lit by thousands of store and streetlights. She looked at a street sign to see the street was named Rose Street. Every lighted sign had the name "Rose." There was Rose Eyes and Ears, Rose Drywall, Rose Delicatessen, Rose Hotel, on and on. She woke, sitting straight up in bed. Ray wanted to know what was going on. What was she dreaming?

She told him and he believed it was about the man in the canoe, traveling in the shipping lanes of the lake. The commercial traffic used designated lanes that were marked on the map of the lake that charted the depths of the water and other things important to travelers. A couple of places on the chart had printed what is called a compass rose. It is important to the navigation of the lake as it contained points, North, East, South, West, and the degrees of the compass. A captain would chart the degree he needed to be heading and then follow that degree on his boat compass.

She and Ray took her dream into the office to figure out the dream vision on the chart of the coast and waters. There was a "Rose" printed directly north of the opening to their marina, in the shipping lane. That's where they believed him to be.

They'd have gone out themselves right then, but the waves hit the shore much too strong. No boat would make it safely out the narrow channel to the lake. They went back to sleep, a prayer on Vi's lips for the lake to calm and the man to stay alive.

At six the next morning, the marine radio crackled alive. "I got him! I got him and he's alive!" a fisherman shouted. They were located in the lake just seven miles east of their harbor near the next creek entering the lake. Vi called the local ambulance.

She wondered how he was doing in the hospital. The reports she'd gotten were positive and his family was celebrating with him. She kind of wished she could be there, but that would be looking for glory or thanks and thanks belonged to God, not her.

Vi knew what she was doing was special. She also believed that doorway to God, that potential that others could also do these things, was great. Psychologist Carl G. Jung talks about developing a Jesus complex, where people in Vi's position came to think of themselves as God. This was never a possibility for Vi. She had no idea what the next message would be or when it would come. If she were God, she'd know these things. When someone had a problem and asked for a dream, the advice that came through was always something she'd never thought about.

Leading others to do the same was the message God had given her the night before in her dreams. She dreamed three times of going to the grand opening of a new department store in town. She actually did it the night before. The same scene was replaying in her mind every time she woke to begin a new dream. She asked God why she dreamt the same scene over and over. A voice said, "I make my money on reruns." He wanted her help reawakening people that this God connection is still there and not just a Bible story. Any enterprise needed exposure and advertising to grow.

What a difference two years can make! Two years before she was beat by business, family, finances and health. Two years ago she made a commitment to do something about her life long nightmares.

Ray came up behind her and put his arms around her. "What are you thinking about?" He asked. After all these years, three children and one grandchild, his touch still made her tingle.

She leaned back against him. "I wish I knew how to tell my story. I've had a physical healing, new exciting opportunities, my life changed around completely. I wish I knew how to help others find the doorway to God that I've found."

"You'll do it." Ray replied with complete faith. "When the time is right, you'll do it."

Vi remembered a piece of advice from somewhere that said, "Watch what you wish for....."

Chapter 2

Two Years Prior
March 1985

This was to be a fun night. Heaven knew they needed some. It had been a long hard winter. It seemed everyone and everything was a fight. Tonight was square dance night. Vi and Ray used to square dance when their children were little. "Being grandparents shouldn't stop us from enjoying that again," Vi thought hopefully. "This new group forming in a neighboring town is exactly the kind of change of pace we need. At least these people are not among those several groups that are trying to get our marina away from us."

Vi remembered a piece of advice from somewhere that said, "watch what you wish for." They'd often talked about owning some little piece of property and being in business for themselves. This desire had led them to jump at the possibility of owning this marina and had been like stepping into a pit of snakes full of envy and greed.

"We need this couple of hours of music and fun," Vi told Ray as she tried to convince him to go. They hadn't done anything but work, worry and fight for a long time.

"If only we'd kept one of our matching costumes we used to dance in, it would make it so much more fun for the new people to see where this can go." Vi replied, beginning to get a little excited about actually going somewhere for fun!

"Who knew we'd be getting back into this after all these years? Let's go!" Ray said.

As they headed out the door and into the car Vi remarked, "The neighbors are probably watching out the window. You'd think it would be too cold to be in a cottage. You notice, they haven't missed a weekend this winter." She couldn't help the fear that crept in whenever she was forced to think of them.

"Yeah, they don't own the road. Just ignore them." Ray wasn't as intimidated, so he said! As they backed the car out of the driveway two couples came bouncing out of the door of the cottage across the street and glared at them leaving. Tears came to Vi's eyes. Ray glanced over a couple of times, not knowing what to say. Finally he said, "Don't let them ruin our evening."

"Why are they doing this?" Vi wanted to know. "I just keep asking myself why."

"They wanted to own the property. Now they plan to make our lives miserable." This was Ray's rationalization of the situation.

"I keep thinking of how hurt and embarrassed I was at the first town meeting on our property." Vi countered, her hurt apparently going deeper inside her.

"That was a year ago, Vi. You have to let it go." Ray said. Frustration still showed in his face, his body language and the tone of his voice. Vi knew he'd bounce up with both fists flying if the opportunity ever came about.

"Mostly," Vi tried to explain her own frustration, "I don't hash it over in my head. But with another meeting coming up next month and watching all their neighborhood meetings that are about us, but don't include us. Why can't they meet on some other road? Meeting in their winter homes is plain intimidation and it's working, with me at least. You go down to the building every day and don't have to see them."

The marina they bought in 1977 was undeveloped land jetties going out into the inland harbor, lots of trees, and some picnic tables in a pavilion and a few docks. Spring brought fishermen, but its cold wet weather still hung on. When they were still friends with the neighbors, they'd all talked with them about closing in the pavilion, adding a side room and a fireplace. Some coffee and light food would serve the fishermen well and add some profitability to the marina.

A building party was arranged and they all worked together to put it up. Dom's two daughters, the neighbors across the street, would work in the snack bar. Another neighbor pitched in to shape hamburgers. The first season was hard, but fun.

Then they learned about building permits.

The town had been offered the property for free before Ray and Vi bought it. The town fathers turned it down. Some people were still upset about that deal and were angry with Ray and Vi because they bought it. The town fathers surely had power over what happened at the marina. They could cause a lot of trouble if they wanted to. Ray and Vi worried what these authorities might do to them.

The trouble, though, came from a totally unexpected source. The ten households of neighbors showed up in a group with a lawyer (a relative just graduated from law school and working for free).

"Vi," Ray's voice brought her back to the present. "You shouldn't have been embarrassed. They should."

"They're too thick skinned to be embarrassed." Vi bit out angrily. She continued as though Ray were the enemy. "They're idiots! What they tried didn't work! To stand there and say they'd taped our phone conversations!"

Her tirade continued. "I'm glad the town attorney spoke up and said that was probably illegal, but why did he wait so long? Why did he let them say all those hurtful things? I keep going over things in my mind. I can't recall anything nasty I said on the phone. I don't think I had nasty in me, till after that night! And to say my kitchen was so dirty I didn't deserve to own a restaurant!"

"They're idiots!" Ray tried to calm her by agreeing with her (which he did) and pointing out the positive. "We got the permit. That's all that matters."

Vi recalled the good people at the meeting. "Thanks to Mr. Richards, some boaters and a few towns people speaking up for us. You and I were too shy or too shocked to speak up for ourselves."

Ray could not accept the possibility of a weakness. "Well that's changed!"

Mr. Richards brought some sense to the whole thing. "Good thing he had the last word." Vi remembered. Mr. Richards owned the only grocery store in town and talked about using this opportunity to build a better tax base for everyone. He pointed out that the neighbors all owned little cheap cottages and paid the majority of their property taxes in another district.

She continued, "Yeah, great for a tax base, where'd they all suddenly get the money to make their cottages year round homes?" The neighbors had soon taken steps to strengthen their position, by moving in full time! "I counted four that can move here anytime they want. That will add to the tax base too."

"Because of this marina." Ray pointed out. "They could only do it because of the marina. This marina is the best and only possibility for big economic growth this town has. Their property values have gone up! What they need is city water piped in. Do these idiots think they'll ever get city water down here by themselves? The home owners on the other lakeshore roads are envious."

As time went by, the battle with the neighbors continued. They hated to walk out the door. Let a stranger appear on their property and Dom was right there seeing who he was. Many times the neighbor's had made fools of themselves calling the DEC and EPA hoping to catch Ray and Vi doing something else without a permit. One brush with authorities had been lesson enough. They made sure they had permits after that. Dredging the channel was the only item that needed a constant permit.

Ray and Vi pulled into the church parking lot and climbed the stairs to the second floor dance hall. The music lightened their spirits and they were eager to get their dancing feet going. The caller shuffled his records, welcomed everyone and asked for a show of hands if anyone had done Western Square Dancing before. Ray and Vi raised their hands and they got put in the first set.

The music started, but suddenly Vi couldn't move. They all stopped. "What's wrong?" Ray asked.

Vi started to panic. "I can't move my legs. I was alright a second ago," Vi said.

"Come sit down," Ray instructed.

"I can't move at all!" Vi pleaded as panic started to cover embarrassment.

A person nearby asked, "Should we call a medic?"

"No, just get me to the car. Take me home! Please!" Vi spoke out.

Chapter 3

Mother's Visits

Vi groaned. She heard the greeting as her mother-in-law came in the front door. Ray's mother had been traveling almost 60 miles nearly every day to take care of Vi, the house and family since Vi was diagnosed with a connective tissue disorder in her blood. Another doctor in the same office called it Rheumatoid Arthritis.

Mother's visits would seem wonderful but, truth is, mother thrived on things like this. She had something to talk about and some defenseless someone to order around. She really wasn't needed. Vi felt Mother's mission was to prove Vi inept at everything. From the day they met, 29 years prior, Vi had never been able to be the person this mother of her husband wanted her to be. A typical argument concerned the brand of window cleaner she used. It had escalated to Vi not caring whether she cleaned the windows or not. Then there were the other, bigger issues.

This mother figure Vi needed in her life was a big disappointment. Her own mother had left when Vi was eight and she had not had much contact with her except for a couple of disastrous years between Vi's age twelve and fourteen. Vi's paternal grandmother had brought her up to respect her elders. Nothing was ever said about fighting for your rights, needing to stick up for yourself when encountering meanness. Vi missed her mother, or the thought of having a mother. Vi overlooked things with her Mother-in-law that she should have stopped, because she was so grateful for this token mother.

There was one place she would draw the line. This woman was not going to drag her naked into the bath tub again! There were a number of ways to accomplish that task without that humiliation!

Vi put her clothes on and met a surprised mother-in-law in the hall.

"I was going to run your bath." Mother said.

"All done," Vi lied. "I'm feeling much better."

"I wish you'd called me." Now Mother tried to put the 'You're inconsiderate' guilts on Vi.

"You're much too fast for me," Vi replied. "The phone works both ways. I didn't know you planned on coming again." Mother moved into the kitchen, made a pot of coffee and put out some cookies she'd brought. Vi followed her and took a seat, trying to stay out of the way.

"How'd the town meeting go? It was last night, wasn't it?" Mother asked.

"It was last night. Ray and the kids went. I felt too sick." Vi replied.

"Well, will they let you move the gas tank?" Mother pushed for details.

"Sure they will." Vi said, warming up to Mother's interest. "Ray said the meeting was a real circus. The neighbors were all there in one group. They walked in with Mr. Brown's nephew, the attorney. Many people turned out and a lot of our boaters came to speak for us. There were so many people they stood along the walls and out into the hall."

Mother was enjoying the story. She loved fights. Vi had to admit she enjoyed this one too, as long as people agreed with her.

Vi continued. "I was talking to my brother's wife and she actually said to me that she could see the neighbor's point of view. To have a big investment like they have and then put a commercial marina on the end of their street…"

"That's probably how they think. It wasn't nice for her to say that," mother said. We agree on that, Vi thought. Mother and Father loved coming to the marina, as did a lot of people.

It was nice when we can talk like this, Vi thought and shared more of her feelings. "It took my breath away that she would say that. And I didn't want to argue with her. I just ended the conversation as fast as I could. The truth is that the marina was here long before the neighbors were. The neighbors mostly bought empty lots and now it's summer cottages. Other people have a right to get to the lake and enjoy it to. Anyone owning this property would want to develop it and they deserve to make a profit on it."

"Well, Sara and Joanne and I were talking and we wondered why you said …" Mother changed the subject.

Here it comes, Vi thought as her good feeling took a dive. We'd been too much like friends for too long this morning. Now I'm being accused of saying something bad.

Historically, Vi's words went from one in-law to another of them. The words got twisted and Vi was the worst person on earth. Vi felt she was in for another argument.

"Mother, not now." Vi said sharply. "I never said anything to be mean to anyone. I'm too sick to discuss this with you now. I'm going back to bed. Thanks for coming."

Mother and Father left in a huff. Father did not have a clue why they were leaving. He'd been fixing to do some fishing. That's a fair sample of Vi and her Mother-in-laws' relationship. Vi usually had to sit and take the verbal beating, which did not happen this time.

Later that day a phone call came that was to change Vi's life for the worse. Ray just happened to be home.

"I'll get it," Ray said as he answered the phone.

"Well greetings to you from the north!" Ray spoke to an evidently friendly person.

"Yes, a break from this cold would be wonderful." What was he saying, who was he talking to? "Yes, we could manage it next week. Nothing going on here and our children will look after everything, feed the dogs, etc." He paused while Vi was jumping out of her seat.

"No, we'll drive. Just give me directions." Ray said. After writing extensively, Ray put down the phone and beamed. "We're going to Florida! Jim and Aggie want us to come for a visit with them. Perfect!"

"Wow, it's like a miracle!" Vi was stunned and pleased, then cautious. "You suppose they've heard about the trouble with the neighbors?"

"Most likely," Ray said, "but they must not be taking sides. At least they want to spend some time with us."

"I'm so excited!" Vi was!

Ray cautioned, "Don't do that. Remember how stress makes you sicker. Good excitement is just as bad as being upset. Stay calm."

"Easy for you to say!" Vi replied.

It'd been a long time since they'd been away from the marina. They both dug into packing and making other arrangements. Ray went to check out the car.

Jim and Aggie were well aware of what was going on, from both sides of the marina dispute. They had a boat in the marina in the summer, were members of the Coast Guard Auxiliary (as were some of the neighbors) and therefore, having spent time with some of the neighbors at meetings and on patrol, they knew the neighbors well. The question was, "How did they feel about what they'd obviously been told by them?" They evidently still liked Ray and Vi enough to invite them down.

The vacation was in a warm climate. This would break the cycle of ice and snow and of mother-in-law visits. The visit gave them a change of scenery away from dodging the stares of the neighbors. It would be their first visit to that part of sunny Florida.

They packed the next day and drove south.

Jim and Aggie were long time boaters in the marina, both retired college professors in the field of health. The four of them walked around the mobile home park where they lived.

Aggie pointed to a little old lady in a wheel chair and said, "We'll pass by her on our way back. Poor thing sits there all day and into the dark hoping someone will stop and talk to her. We'll introduce you on the way back."

The visit was delightful. The poor thing beamed from the attention. Vi became curious, as they all excused themselves and started to walk away.

"What's wrong with her?" Vi asked.

"She has Rheumatoid Arthritis," Aggie replied.

That last hit Ray and Vi like a ton of bricks. They exchanged surprised glances. Neither knew anything about the disease. To think it led to being crippled and in a wheel chair!

The next morning Vi was sick with a bad flu, all the nasty symptoms. It seems the potential for flu sometimes sits and waits for you to let your defenses down. Vi had done that the night before with the realization of her future. Vi spent the rest of the week there in bed. She urged Ray and the others to get out of the house and have some fun. They could see some of the area.

The only request Vi made was, "Would you please pick me up

some books on Rheumatoid Arthritis?"

Jim was quick to point out, "One thir
are the many people trying to take advantaʃ
you books."

"Yes, but I need to understand what's going
handle it," agreed Vi.

Aggie said, "We'll help him pick out some good ones and we
can copy off some things from our textbooks too."

"Thank you so much!" Vi replied.

All Vi could see was that lady in the wheel chair. She had to
learn as much as she could about the disease.

The power of stress was one thing she picked up on with all
the advice she was to read. Vi felt the consequences of the experience.
Maybe she could avoid some of the conflict at home that caused the
stress by putting it all on Ray's shoulders. Maybe she could find
something to do rather than worry about the neighbors, the towns
people, the mother-in-law and various family members, the hoodlum
who came and tried to get the marina away from them by opening a
suitcase filled with $30,000.00 in cash, because most small business
people fail and he was offering just what they'd put down on the
property. How'd he know that, she wondered. Even sick as she was
these thoughts crept in and upset her.

They heard rumblings of dissatisfaction from the yacht club
about the way Ray and Vi ran the place. A few were leaving for
another harbor. Someone was stirring them up. It was probably the
neighbor across the street.

Maybe Vi could let her daughter move to an apartment to save
arguments there. They could probably afford to pay for it. It may not
be morally right but it was a lot easier than handling the constant
battles with her. Maybe Vi should resign from the County Tourism
Board. That could be a bad business move, Vi thought.

Maybe, maybe, maybe, but one thing seemed impossible. How
could she get rid of her constant nightmares? That, along with the lack
of sleep it brought, was a sure source of stress. Maybe this was the
original source of her stress. Someone had to know and maybe written
about dreams somewhere. Maybe the first stop when getting home
was a trip to the bookstore. It was time to find out what others knew
about dreams!

" The first thing that sank in was
that dream messages come
from God. They come
to heal and make
your life whole.."

Chapter 4

Edgar Cayce On Dreams

Almost home, they made a stop to pick up a book on dreams. Vi had to know what other people knew about dreams. The only book on the shelves was "Edgar Cayce On Dreams."

It was in an obscure corner of the store along with psychic stuff. Vi had a moment of panic that this was not an accepted subject. What would the clerk think? Was it someone she knew? Thank God not! Still, she had to know. Other people had led her life, told her what to think long enough. She bought the book and was reading it before they got home.

The first thing that sank in was that dream messages come from God. They come to heal and make your life whole. Edgar Cayce had spent his lifetime solving other people's problems, health, jobs, relationships and more by going into a trance and having their question read to him. At age 17, a vision helped him overcome his own health problem. In a trance state Cayce could even tell you why you'd come into this world and what your goal should be. It seems we have a purpose for being in this life.

Vi thought about that. She'd raised three wonderful children who hadn't caused anyone else any trouble. That goal, raising her children, if that was her life's goal, was extremely important. It seemed to be accomplished at this point in her life.

Maybe there was more. Whatever it was, being sick and crippled hardly seemed a worthwhile endeavor. If only Cayce were still alive. A question was read to Cayce, while he was in a trance. Cayce gave readings that told what medicine to take and where to find the medicine. Cayce told why a person came into this world at this time (he said we live on earth more than once). He was able to tell who had been in one's life before and explained what may be the cause of one's problems this time.

Vi wondered if Ray's mother had been with her in a past lifetime. What did she do to her that might be carried forward to this lifetime? They sure seemed destined to make each other's lives miserable. Then there were all these other people problems. Vi thought, "I must have been a dictator and wiped out a whole generation! There are a few I'd like to wipe out now!"

There were directions to put a pad of paper next to her bed, drink a large glass of water before turning in for the night, and to tell herself, I will remember my dreams. I will remember my dreams. The first few nights Vi got nothing. She'd wake up. As soon as she moved her arm, the dreams flitted away.

What about the trance Cayce went into? Cayce said regular meditation deepened your spiritual life, made dreams more productive. Could she do that? She read books on self-hypnosis and meditation. They turned out to be one and the same. Actually, they reminded her of the method she used successfully to rid herself of migraine headaches.

She'd suffered horrible migraines for years. She'd be bed bound for twenty-four hours each time, not able to drive for the pain and spots before her eyes. The University of Rochester was conducting research on biofeedback and migraines. There was an article in the paper that said electrodes were attached to people's fingertips to get them thinking of warm fingertips. The idea was to bring the blood away from the base of the skull and into the hands, relieve the pressure on the brain.

Not having access to the electrodes, Vi chose the next best thing to making her fingers warm and pulling the blood down, mittens. It worked wonderfully. At the onset of symptoms Vi donned gloves and thought fingers. The migraines never manifested.

Vi lost her fear of the migraines and the migraines disappeared. There was more to this mind over matter thing than she knew and she vowed to try meditation to help cure her nightmares.

When ready, she waited till everyone was busy elsewhere, put the dogs out, locked the doors, unplugged the phone and put her pad beside the living room couch. Feeling very frustrated she lay on the couch, wiped away the tears, and called out to God in her mind. "Why God? Why did you put me on this earth? Life hasn't been so good so far. Ray and the children are fine, but money's always a problem, my childhood was bad and now I'm to spend the rest of my life as a cripple? Why did you put me on this earth anyway?"

Instantly visions came into her mind, so many she couldn't remember them all. When she was done, she was sure she'd seen visions of talents. She was able to remember three, singing, photography and writing. She wrote them down.

Vi always enjoyed singing. No one else enjoyed her singing. Writing was out. Photography had been a hobby she recently decided to give up. It just cost money. She had an expensive camera and had planned to sell it. She put that plan on hold for a while to see what came of this vision. Thinking it over, sure she'd had a message from God; she decided to use all three talents.

She unlocked the doors, turned on the phone and turned the marine radio back on to hear a person with a funny sounding boat name calling another boat. Something like, 'Big Wind calling Tony's Toy.' Naughty, but funny thoughts, came to mind and Vi took her pad and wrote a story using the various boat names she'd heard. The story was all boat names telling their own story. No other words in between. It was so clever she put it into the computer. If nothing else, she'd had a block of time with no stress, just fun. Maybe that's what this is all about, she thought.

Next, she put a country western tape in the player and marched to the music around the dining room table. She sang as loud as she wanted, everyone else in the household was out working in the marina. She pampered the swelling that came up after the exercise, but at least she'd gotten some exercise. What fun! She could do this!

Over the next few days she went from walking a few feet at a time to being able to walk to the end of their two-car driveway and back! Best yet, she began to capture her dreams!

At first it was only a feeling she wrote down. When she woke with one word in mind, she wrote that. One morning that word was beans. She included some with their supper that night.

Vi had a feeling she should tell the source of her dreams, I've ignored you before, but not anymore. I'm acting on whatever I see. Words came to her, "I'll never tell you to do anything bad. Interpret the symbols!"

One night, in a dream, she had a vivid experience of preparing a chocolate ice cream sundae complete with whipped cream, nuts and a cherry. She ran the spoon around the edge catching some vanilla ice cream and some chocolate syrup and raised it to her lips. Just as she opened her mouth and was to put the delectable spoonful in, the chocolate turned to a horde of ants. Gagging, she woke and wrote the incident on her dream pad. It was a long time before she wanted to eat anything like that.

In one dream she was in a restaurant standing in line to pay her bill. When her time came, she pulled lettuce leaves out of her pocket. Waking and writing, she made a vow to add more lettuce to her diet.

Once having dreamed of tuna fish in a can turning into cat food as it came to her lips, she lessoned up the amount of tuna she was eating.

In yet another dream she was driving a car across the border from Canada to the US and was stopped by Border Patrol. They asked to look in her trunk. There they found illegal hams. She caught the pun immediately. Loose weight! Get the fat out of her trunk.

So began her new routine of dreams, diet and exercise. Often times, just waking up, getting out of bed, brought lots of pain and swelling in her joints. Writing was a nice sit-down diversion. She wrote as many stories using boat names as she could and marched each day, sometimes twice a day around that table. When you think God is telling you to do something, you do it.

She recorded her dreams and always tried to find a message in them. Sometimes it was easy. Other times, when she did not understand them, during the day she'd hear the same words come out of another source, like a conversation with someone or in a book or from the TV. She knew she'd had a message and what it was.

There were other ways to honor her dreams. When she had a dream of elephants, she took that as a comment on her weight and just in case it was something else, she brought out a small toy elephant and used it as a knick-knack near her bed. She was starting a collection of dream images.

She'd spent many years ignoring God; now she did all she could to convince Him of her seriousness in changing her life to the way He needed it to be. Although her body was full of pain, the hope, the music, the writing were putting her emotions on a more stable level. She once heard a voice in her dreams say; "to have fear was not to have God in her life". She recognized it as a passage from the

Bible. She looked it up and tried to remind herself of that whenever fear crept in.

She'd spent years ignoring her health. Someone once told her, "You rebuild your body cell by cell and it takes seven years to replace all of the cells." If she was going to be alive seven years from now, and she thought she would, she might as well grow the healthiest cells she could. She needed to avoid the heart problems and diabetes that had caused her parents early deaths.

Reading the paper one day in August she stumbled on an article about a self-help class put on by the Arthritis Foundation in the next county. She joined. She learned a lot that was valuable and became it's representative in her own county, adding home visits to other sick people to her schedule.

It struck Vi how some women became the disease. It's like they had no life before arthritis. Their total identity was "Marie, the arthritic." That's how they saw themselves and Vi realized how self-defeating that was. The Arthritis Foundation had a tape of meditation for healing that she taught the women to use. This meditation for healing thing was proven enough to be used by the Arthritis Foundation. This proved to her that this mind over matter attitude about healing was on the right track.

Some nightmares still bothered her. Between 10 P.M. and 11:30 P.M., when Ray finally came to bed, violent beings terrorized her. She often ran silently screaming out to cuddle next to Ray. When Ray was beside her they weren't there. She'd made a lot of changes in her life. She couldn't help wonder why God was allowing this to happen to her!

Finally, she could take it no more. When it happened again, Vi kneeled in her bed and pleaded with God to put a stop to this.

Vi prayed out loud, "We've worked together! You tell me to change something and I do! Take these demons away! If there's more to change, you know I will! That's it! Take them away!" She lay her head back down on the pillow and went to sleep. The beings never came back.

To her, this was all about God. Maybe if she went back to church, things would get better.

Vi had raised her children in the Methodist Church, been a Sunday School Teacher. She and Ray were Youth Group leaders. Vi was a registered Lay leader and sometimes gave a sermon. She'd not been steady about her attendance with the kids out of school and the purchase of the marina. Ray didn't see a need to go.

She started back by herself, joined the Bible study group and the choir. She wanted Bible study because there might be a clue there as to what was happening to her through the dreams and why? She wanted to know more about the book. Wanted to be able to answer those who said what she was doing was wrong or impossible. She wanted to know more about the people of the Bible who'd had dreams.

She talked it over with the minister. He'd come to visit a couple of times. She told him of her dreams, but it was new to him. He'd joined the ministry because of a spiritual experience he'd had, but told her now he never talked of it because people in the church were not ready for the truth. Vi got the message.

She didn't keep quiet. The woman in charge of the Sunday school declared an instant war in that this had to be the work of the devil. Talk of hypocrisy! She wanted Vi to be able to help her own son get rid of his nightmares. When Vi had no insight on this, Vi was damned and talked about.

This was not the place for Vi to find answers. She then went to the Lutheran Church, joined in the choir there. One dream came where Vi was in the choir loft waiting for the others to show. She turned around and saw a blackboard behind her. Written on it were the words "Why are you here? You're psychic." As much as she didn't want to be called psychic, the handwriting was on the wall. She left that church also.

Still, she had no doubts where her faith lay. To her it was more than faith. It was a knowing. Reading the Bible once more, she came across the words "everything good comes from God." She knew this was good. She knew this was from God. But why her? How could He spend so much time with her? The only place left to seek answers was the Catholic Church. That night she had a dream of several nuns sitting around a conference table. She called the church twice and went there once. No one opened the door or answered the phone. It must be something <u>she</u> knew about Catholics.

The answer came! They believed in, talked to, prayed to angels. Vi could accept that an angel would have the time for her. This put her mind at ease. When reading the Bible and other books she read, "All is one. All good comes from God." She went back to saying and thinking, "God is talking to me." She kept telling everyone about her dreams.

Still she was the bookkeeper of the business and the money situation lay heavy on her mind. Not everything had been made better. God was making Vi earn her better life!

One possibility about money came clear. The guy that sewed the canvas tops for the boaters was much in demand, not only in this harbor, but others as well. Sewing was something Vi could do and she was feeling so much better. They got a deal on a commercial sewing machine, the guys built long tables in the empty walkout basement and Vi went to work measuring, cutting and sewing. She'd made most of the children's clothes as they grew up. Her Grandmother and school home-economics teacher had taught her well.

She found a couple of boaters willing to let her practice on their boats for a big reduction in price. One problem remained, tugging the heavy canvas material made her back and shoulders hurt. It wasn't long before Vi knew this wasn't going to work.

They put an ad in the local paper to sell the equipment. It sold quickly and Vi and Ray watched sadly as the new owners stripped their basement of all the equipment and inventory. When it was all gone, she walked to the mailbox.

One big lesson, about to be brought home to Vi, was God's timing. A surprise waited for her there that very day the canvas business was being driven down the road.

The only mail that day was a brochure from someone starting a local sports magazine. He wanted advertisers, but he also wanted writers. "Well, boating is a sport," she thought. "I'll send him one of my stories."

Within a week the man called. He loved the story. He said that Vi was a natural born writer and he wanted a story like that for each paper. Maybe other boating subjects as well. Vi's head could have burst, her ego got so big. She pulled out a piece she'd written on the proper use of the marine radio, went to town, bought a Writer's Digest Magazine to see how to submit pieces to regular magazines. It said to send to one magazine at a time, wait to hear from them and if rejected, then send to another. She looked up boating magazines in the library and came up with eight. She decided to send to all eight at one time.

She didn't figure she had any more time to waste if this was to be her path.

Vi took a quick look back in her dream journal and found a dream where she was getting something out of the mailbox. If only she'd known enough to wait.

She heard from one magazine berating her for not following the rules. Seems they owned more than one magazine. However, a phone call came from a publisher at Lakeland Boating Magazine. He bought her article and asked if she would write travel pieces about ports around Lake Ontario. He could also use some pictures with the articles! Of course! Two of her talents!

"How about one on Toronto Harbor?" she asked, "I've been there many times."

"Just what I had in mind." The publisher replied. "You might want to call on the tourism director there for any new plans they might be considering. His name is _____ and his phone number is _____. Two months give you enough time?"

"I can have it in two weeks." Vi was sure.

The publisher was firm. "Two months will be soon enough. We might want rewrites or have questions. How about Coburg the month after that?"

"That'll keep me busy," Vi said excitedly! She couldn't wait to tell Ray and anyone else who'd listen.

Toronto Harbor was a favorite destination for boaters out of Vi's marina. Ray and Vi had been there a couple of times themselves. She had photos from a trip they'd made there. She thought back to that first trip across the lake and remembered how traveling there by boat the first time was intimidating. You're going into a foreign country wondering where to check in with customs. How do you find the entrance to the harbor, where do you tie up, what's to see? These were questions they often got from boaters making their first trips there.

Vi put herself in that first time position once again and described the compass points, the view of the coastline from the lake both east and west of the harbor, in case you didn't land exactly where you needed to be and all the rest of the stuff. In viewing her photos, she decided to take a car trip around the end of the lake to get some fresh photos from Toronto Island of Toronto's skyline at night. Still not satisfied, she talked her way onto a boat whose owners patiently let her take other pictures for a mention in the magazine.

Still not confident of her ability, she called on an acquaintance she'd recently made to proof read the article. Phyllis was the public relations person in a nearby hospital. Vi had been asked to represent the Arthritis Foundation at a health fair there and this had led to new friend, Phyllis. Phyllis was an English major in college and had taught some writing courses. Over lunch she read the piece. Being a sailor, she also had some knowledge of the subject.

The funniest thing happened. Zip, zip, zip, Phyllis marked off paragraphs and indicated a move to another part of the paper. She advised Vi that after writing an article to cut out each paragraph and move them around until the piece flowed more smoothly. What a gift that was. Cayce, or someone said, "When the student was ready, the teacher will come."

"There are lots of people like me who can edit your work," Phyllis said. "The world needs people with ideas, like yours. Just write. I'll help you."

Vi had a new career and a new way of thinking about herself. The publisher had a list of ports. He wanted articles and photos on each, even some on Lake Erie. One call from the publisher put her in touch with the producer of a TV program, Great Lakes Boater. She got that writing job also. She even picked up some money reporting on town board meetings for three towns and she had a few feature articles in the local newspaper.

If only she'd waited for something in the mailbox rather than starting that canvas business. Having found the value of rereading old dreams, Vi spent some time going back over her journal. She pasted in the scraps of paper she had written dreams on before starting the notebook. Recently, she'd seen a ferry sinking with many people going to their death. There was an article she cut out of the paper a couple of days later where just such a thing had happened in the Mediterranean Sea. She wondered why she'd seen it.

Another dream, early on, had been about her daughter, at a young age, having to be tracked down and a knife taken away from her. She was out to kill Japanese people. Then there was the clipping about the hijacking of a Japanese airliner by a person with a knife.

Amongst her readings was the theory that intelligence encircled the earth like ether. In the night, in meditation and musings we could tap into that ether, see things happening far away whether they pertained to us or not. Scientists, artists, writers often got ideas there. That would explain why sometimes more than one person came up with the same idea. Carl Jung spoke of the collective unconscious in much the same way. The difference was that the doorway was within. Thinking it over, whether circling the earth or within, the path to reaching this source was the same, dreams, meditation and musings.

The predictions that held personal meaning for her, she knew came from a heavenly helper. With warnings she had a chance to change the outcome. Her dream guide, or God, wanted to save her stress and illness. If changing the outcome was not possible, she could at least be the strong one in the group, like at a funeral, because the shock had come in the dream, before the happening. And she knew it was meant to be.

The predictions were part of what kept her faithful to this process. They added to the mystery of life. Who was telling her, why her and what would she be told next? When a nightmare came she'd write it down to decipher later and then go back to sleep, repeating the Lord's Prayer.

By that second summer all her talents were at work with two of them making money. Singing had led to a Sweet Adeline's Barbershop group. When you are singing you are not being negative. In Vi's case, this was better than money.

Vi's dreams had shown her a record being cut. As a child she'd witnessed a new record being made on a home machine. In her dream she'd seen the needle cutting a groove and the white plastic that came curling out of the groove, the old empty stuff floated away into the wind.

She read or heard somewhere that our life is a record. In those grooves is everything we do, think and feel. The amount of time we spend on negative things is in that groove.

The record plays over and over. If negativity is recorded there, we experience negativity again and again. What we live and think is what we bring more of to us. We can recut that record; erase the negativity by things like singing. As happy thoughts take over more of your record of life, you become a happy person. What you are is what you draw to you. If you are negative, you draw bad experiences. If you are happy, you draw good things. It is also wise to empty those thoughts occasionally to let God's needs for you come into your life.

The amount of time Vi spent singing, listening to music, writing and laughing with friends was time used to turn her life around.

One recurring dream image she began to have was of being in her Grandmother's attic, going through chests of stuff. She'd often done this as a child. In one dream dictionary she had likened the image to finding treasures in our mind. These treasures held the possibilities of the good that could be in your life if you made room. Vi wanted some good!

Another dream showed her preparing for a wedding. This is a good sign, a sign of meeting on a common ground, a celebration, and a reward. After some discussion, in the dream, they decided to go into an old school building; there were many valuable items to be found. Two rows of children tried to block their way, but finally let them pass. One stipulation was not to take any of the old furniture out of the rooms. The building was square with rooms on all outside walls, a hall around the inside of these rooms and another block of unknown space in the middle.

They looked and marveled at all the antique treasures in the rooms. Leaving the building they looked back to see a tower in the middle. The stairway to the tower was in the middle. When they had opened the door a voice said, "Do not come up here." Now they saw a brilliant green (the color of healing) emerald sparkled in the tower window. The jewel was energy waiting for discovery.

The building was Vi. The treasures were buried inside Vi's unconscious. The message was to bring them out, don't be a child forever guarding them. Think of the learning that could take place when the rooms were cleaned out and the treasures put to good use. Perhaps the emerald center, her true self would be available then. In other words, do the dream work! Bring out the buried treasures to make your life easier, more individuated.

Sometimes something is glaringly missing from a dream story, that could be a clue to it's meaning. She also considered what the opposite action might be saying. Keep the old issues of childhood buried. Then there would be no empty space to fill with new experiences. Then the doorway to healing would surely stay blocked. The truth always rings that ah-ha bell deep inside. And Vi knew to work on those old childhood issues now.

The dreams were helpful, productive and wonderful. The pain still persisted. Vi walked with a cane a lot of the time. That was part of the disease. Her goal was to stay away from the other illnesses that were in her family.

Otherwise things were good. She'd lost a lot of weight and had little time to worry about the neighbors and now knew they envied her position as the local published Lake Ontario expert. They couldn't take that away! When you concentrate on God's purpose for you, you develop things no one can take away!

Chapter 5

I Will Dream For You

Vi still had marina duties. She walked down to the gas dock to read the pump and found herself in a deep conversation with a lady she liked who didn't dock her boat there, but lived a short way east along the coastline. Sandy and her husband, Tom, were members of another Coast Guard Auxiliary. They often stopped by and took Ray and Vi off on a pleasant boat rides.

"Vi, you've lost weight! And you're smiling! What a difference from last time we were here. Are you still dreaming?" Sandy wanted to know.

"Have I got stories to tell you!" Vi replied. "I'm getting all kinds of messages in my dreams. I wake up and write down a dream and next day the same words come out of someone's mouth. Sometimes it's a person in the marina, sometimes a person on the radio or TV and sometimes it's written in a book I read. I take that as a health message and see what change I can make. Cayce says that nothing happens by chance. It's telling me to change something."

"What about the nightmares?" Sandy asked.

Vi replied, "Hardly ever a nightmare. It was like the nightmares had been telling me to <u>pay attention</u>! Now I'm getting some long stories."

"Like what?" Sandy asked.

"Well, last night is a good example." Vi relaxed and was happy to have someone to share this with. "Let's walk over by a picnic table. The dream was so vivid I almost threw up."

They settled on a bench and Vi continued, "It took me back to my childhood. I spent a couple of years with my mother on a farm. Step dad was a tenant farmer. My little brother and I were given newborn calves to nurse with bottles. We spent a lot of time with them. We'd push on their foreheads and they'd playfully push back. They became our living dolls. We named them! Then one day, the pets appeared on our supper table. We felt so sick! We were made to eat the meat, but a lot went under the table to the dog!"

"Wow," said Sandy, "it must have been like living it over again."

"It <u>was</u> living it over again! I've got to do something about it!" Vi said.

"What do you think it meant?" Sandy was curious.

"I'm giving up beef. Other people do it. That couple over there are vegetarians," Vi said. "You wouldn't believe this, but they stopped me this morning and started telling about when they stopped eating beef. I didn't even ask them."

"Did you see the morning news about Canadians not wanting our beef?" Sandy asked.

Vi knew and said, "That's another thing. It's a message. I know it is."

"What about Ray and the kids?" Sandy asked. "Will they give up beef, too?"

Vi replied, "No. I'll cook beef for them when they want it. I'll have something else for me. When God tells you something, you do it. It won't be hard."

"Can you dream for me?" Sandy asked.

"You're crazy! It doesn't work that way!" This time Vi was surprised.

"Just try it." Sandy seemed sure. "I need to know if I'll be retiring from Kodak soon. We've got some investments that need moving around and I need to know."

"Sandy, I wish I could, but I never heard of such a thing." Vi was laughing.

Sandy's husband, Tom, was waving for her to come back to the boat. They were gassed and ready to go.

"Oh," Sandy said, "we're taking a two day trip across the lake to Coburg tomorrow. You and Ray want to go with us?"

"Great!" Vi exclaimed. "I can't imagine Ray saying no and we'll be back before the weekend – won't we?"

"Sure, Vi. Talk to you tomorrow." Sandy left and Vi continued on her way back up to the house thinking about the beef dream and the other changes. The neighbors were in their yard across the street. One would think they'd rather spend their time on the lakeside of their house. They have no one to drive crazy over there.

Slipping inside, Vi went straight to the kitchen to prepare two suppers, one for her, a beef one for Ray, Ron and Joy.

That night Vi had forgotten the talk with Sandy about her possible retirement, but the Spirit who came in her dreams had not. Just as she laid her head back on her pillow in the dark room and closed her eyes, she heard the sound of roller skates on a wood floor. Loud! Then Sandy came barreling around a corner on the skates, making a quick stop. She wore a huge grin and carried a sign that said, RETIRED!!!

Vi laughed, put on the light and wrote the vision on her pad by the bed.

Sandy phoned the next morning to say they were leaving their dock and would be there in about fifteen minutes. Vi told her, "I think your retirement might be coming through faster than you think," "You roller skated into my dream carrying this retired sign. I didn't think about it after we talked. I was too excited about going to Canada today. That dream vision was so neat."

Sandy replied, "Thank you so much, Vi. Tom is going to ask you for a dream while we're away. The weather report is good and the lake looks like a piece of glass. We'll be across in a couple of hours."

Tom wanted to know if he should sell his 34-foot cruiser and buy a larger yacht. If they did, they would sell their house and move on board the yacht full time. Summers they'd spend in the Rochester area and winters traveling down south.

That night in Coburg on board Tom and Sandy's boat, Vi's dream had them in a really large boat, cruising around some islands, going under a bridge and back out to sea. Dolphins porpoised next to their boat, the sun shown and everything was picture perfect. Little did she know she and Ray would be on that boat sharing Christmas dinner with them years later as they traveled around Clearwater Island in Florida.

Now Vi knew. She could dream for other people.

As soon as Phyllis heard, she wanted a dream.

"You've got to keep this strictly between us," Phyllis begged. "I haven't told a soul. I'm thinking of running for Mayor of Medina. Will you dream for me and let me know what God says?"

That night, Vi held a piece of paper with Phyllis's name

address, phone number, and her question. That night, Vi saw stars filling a dark sky with millions of stars. She wrote that down. Vi thought that it must mean sky's the limit.

Vi thought for a moment and said to herself, "Or it might be, 'In your dreams.'"

The only dream was a little frightening. She watched a parade from a second floor rooftop outside a bedroom window. She had to be careful not to slip. An old lady lay in the bed inside. Here comes the parade. Leading off is a huge army tank. A person was strapped to each track of the tank, going round, round, under the tank, and back up over the top, all down the street. People cheered.

Vi called Phyllis the next morning and told her the dream.

"That's what I saw, Phyllis. I think the answer is yes, but don't slip off the roof."

Phyllis replied thoughtfully. "You might be right. Guess God wants us to make our own decisions, but He's pointing out some traps here. Being tied to that track and putting on a show for the people is a lot like politics. I'm not sure I'm ready for that."

"What about the old lady sleeping in the bed?" Vi asked.

Phyllis laughed and said, "My grandmother lived on Main Street when she was alive. We often watched parades from her window. She always said not to go out on the roof. We might slip."

This was an example of synchronicity. Like a verification the dream was for Phyllis, something Vi had not known about Phyllis that came in the dream.

A friend of Phyllis' called the next week and wanted a dream.

She introduced herself as Gail. "Vi, I'm thinking about leaving my husband of twenty years. He hardly ever comes home anymore. I've tried keeping beer for him in the refrigerator, but that makes no difference. When he does come home, he's drunk, angry, not a nice person. Will you ask God what I'm supposed to do? I was raised to take my vows seriously, but I can't live like this."

"I'll give it a try," Vi promised.

Vi thought she'd better caution Gail, "You need to know, I have very strong opinions on this. I may not be able to set my own feelings aside."

Vi paused and continued to say, "I'll say no more and try. It'll be interesting to see what comes in the dreams."

Vi had very strong personal feelings concerning abuse of any kind. When she said beer, her mind jumped to abuse. For a short time, when she was a small child, an aunt and uncle lived with her. After two of their drunken fights, and Vi cowering under a bed, her parents made them leave. If she'd been asked for advice, she would have told Gail to get out of the house and the marriage, fast. Their nighttime guides had a different view.

Vi put a note under her pillow. She had a question to ask God. It's almost like programming your dreams. You ask a question and the answers are more forthright. She found the first dream often restates the problem. Spirit seems to be confirming that the night's dreams are for her.

Dream #1 had her trudging through a hot dry desert, searching, following a path of many footsteps before her. The path went from oasis to oasis. Communities were built up around each oasis, but she would re-enter the desert again each time. The path was a circle that kept bringing her back to the oasis where her husband danced with girl after girl.

Gail's life was like a desert, dry, hot and empty. In spite of other oases (places to rest and live) she always came back to her husband. Based on Vi's concept of him, she thought the girls might be bottles of beer.

Dream #2 took place in a big hotel. The President of the U.S. (the first Mr. George Bush) is scheduled to appear on stage. Gail, head of the toy department, gets to stand with him. She is completely covered with fabric; the letters of his name are printed down her sleeve. We are all very proud of her.

He comes on stage and does some acrobatics. Afterward, he wants to purchase a toy. Gail waits on him. She is in charge of toys and should be thrilled to wait on this important person. She is shocked when he wants special privileges, like not paying. She's also shocked that he wants toys not yet on the shelves. She refuses to help him.

It seemed Gail had a problem involving people she should look up to, respect. The President was an authority figure, and she had a problem with his lack of honesty.

On the other hand, she may have been placing too much importance in the wrong area and was now questioning her perception of authority. Questioning authority is questioning the meaning of life.

This dream contained a health warning, also, advice to put some fun into her life. Gail was shown in charge of the department (of her life). In this case, it was a toy department. This was interesting and complicated. Vi decided to write it all in a letter to Gail. In the letter, explaining the dreams, Vi asked her if she'd had any fun lately.

She was shown on the stage of her life, angels watched her and applauded her. She was doing something right. She was wearing her beliefs on her sleeve for all to see. Remember the letters? She needed to stand for her beliefs.

The angels were proud she had begun the search that would draw her closer to what God wanted for her.

The last dream, dream #3, held the clue to seeing the problem from the right perspective and the solution God wanted her to follow.

In the dream, Gail and her husband were driving around a busy city watching gangs tear apart cars with tire irons. They finally find two police cars and tell them of the problem. Somehow Gail gets outside the car and her husband stops to let her back inside. He would not leave her behind. The tire blows and Vi saw them both outside their car, on a dark street, trying to figure out what to do with the flat tire.

A rich foreign tourist comes into the dream. He passes them with his entourage. Gail tries to explain who he is to her husband. She believes it is Crocodile Dundee because of his Australian accent. He gives them a note, but they can't read a word of it. He wrote in a language foreign to them.

It seemed her husband loved her. The car represented their journey through life. He came back for her in the dream and let her back in the car. They were standing together trying to solve the flat tire problem and, of course, flat tires, like their relationship, could be fixed.

Why did the rich foreign tourist hand them a note written in another language? Were she and her husband not speaking the same language in their lives? Or, perhaps, it was something about the fact that no matter how smart you are, there is some place in this world you can travel and not know the language. Vi hoped Gail could make sense of it.

Since the dreams were from Gail's mind, she could see the truths better than Vi could. This is where the synchronicity, a shocker of truth, came through.

Gail knew the message was about her husband's dyslexia. His own dissatisfaction with life was based on this one fact and had nothing to do with his feelings for her. Gail felt she needed to be more understanding of him and work on herself. They could fix the "flat tire" of their marriage.

Over time, Gail was to find her husband telling the next door neighbor that he'd fallen back in love with his wife.

Gail felt the dreams of oasis after oasis talked about both her husband and her father having had drinking problems. Dream #1, she said, was "right on." She has a co-dependency problem with alcoholics.

She feels, now, in a husband-wife situation, she can break this pattern and work more on her own life. After sharing these dreams, she decided to stay with her husband. Things greatly improved. A year later she wrote back, "I won't have to face this challenge again."

Regarding the second dream, Gail wrote, "Honesty has always been a real bug of mine. I hated dishonesty and everything was either black or white (hence the reference to the president trying to get something for nothing). There is a large gray area now. Not that I can be dishonest with others or myself. I've learned to look behind the dishonesty and see their reason, usually fear.

"As far as toys," Gail continued, "you were right on target again. I never really learned to 'play'. There was too much discord the first seven years of my life and I took the very serious role of being the good girl and not doing anything wrong - high achiever - hard on myself, etc.

"Now I play more. I paint even if there's vacuuming to do - because I want to and my husband helps me with the laundry and cleaning! I'm still too serious, but I'm 'becoming'!"

Her health message, the part about the toys, prompted her to take precautions. She took a heart stress test, which showed potential problems and she was able to overcome them.

Gail said she felt God had touched her. When you open your mind to this, miracles walk in. Gail joined a Children of Alcoholics group and found herself in the hands of a psychologist with a strong spiritual connection who has been a tremendous help to her.

Besides working as a dental assistant, Gail took up art and

joined a singing group, which travels extensively.   She and her husband began camping together. Their relationship has turned around completely.

Gail is considering becoming a minister.   God led her transformation and her husband became her strongest supporter.

Chapter 6

The Friendly Side Of Demons

Life was changing for Vi. She was hearing her Creator's voice. Hearing and understanding are two different things. She had gone off in so many directions on her own, she now had big lessons to learn to pull her back to her purpose. The good news is that she was listening.

Pain ruled her day. Vi thought back to her last nightmare and actually had to check her calendar. The nightmares are becoming less.

Snakes are an archetype (myth, universal story) that one's instinct dredges up to tell you something. The instinct for Vi to be true to herself was strong. It bubbled up in her dreams as demons chasing her, as old mythological stories of who she could be. Vi had been denying her self-worth due to years of conditioning. She was always trying to be the good girl, but she failed at several things. She seemed unable to please anyone.

Now, more often, she woke with a pleasant story in her mind and came to believe the story on waking was wishful thinking. She believed it was who she could be if she made the right decisions. She later learned it was the dream world compensating for what she had or was working toward in her life. Her aim was too low.

Changes needed to come to bring any of those good things forward into her waking life. Her persona, the Vi she showed to the world, had to change. She needed confidence. How do you get that? Her ego, her waking thoughts of who she was had to die to give way to the new Vi. This brought dream scenes of death. The change she needed happened in small steps. As Jeremy Taylor says, the little girl who can't tie her shoes must die before the little girl who can tie her shoes can come into being.

Vi had to loose her fear of talking about herself. She had to find value in who she is. She had to find power over certain situations and use it. One waking clue available to her was to concentrate on what came easy to her. The adventure of the dreams goes beyond the snakes, but snakes are a good place to begin.

At one point, she thought her usual demons, snakes, seemed to be turning into friends. She told me, "A short time ago, if I was feeling depressed or guilty about something, snakes would appear in my dreams like punishment. I'd be hurt by a bad experience during the day and then I'd feel punished again when the snakes appeared. It hardly seemed fair. But that wasn't what was happening. My special calendar has made a few things a lot clearer."

Vi had been charting the snakes and all her dreams on a calendar, trying to see what things, during the day, brought her punishment at night. Maybe, if she understood better what angered God, she could change. She was sure the snakes coincided with arguments, but which, with whom and why?

She color-coded one side of that day's calendar block, black for bad dreams and black for a bad day on the other side of the square. Just in case it was something she ate or saw on TV, she made a note of these in her dream journal for each date, to be compared with the calendar when a nightmare did come.

She color-coded happy days and happy dreams in yellow. If she felt particularly touched by Spirit, she made that day or dream blue. When she had a message about health and had a better than average healthy day, that day got a green. There was definitely a connection between her dreams and what happened in the next day.

One of those Jungian synchronicities (or meaningful coincidences) was that she was using a calendar with the moon changes printed on it. A different moon sign, Aries, Sagittarius, etc., comes into dominant position every three days. She found the phases of the moon played a part in her life also. Maybe there was more to this horoscope thing than she knew.

Her own birth sign, the Pisces, gave her the most consistent trouble. Every time that rolled around, life seemed particularly out of control. She'd wake in a bad mood. Things would fall from her hands creating messes. It was a day that if anything could go wrong, it would go wrong.

Ray watched this phenomenon with her. As one Pisces day approached, they decided to take things into their own hands by getting away from home. Getting in the car and taking a long ride was something they both enjoyed. They had a wonderful day. Not even knowing it could be done, they broke a pattern. The demons of that moon period never returned. There were other black marks.

Then she noticed it wasn't just arguments or just a certain person. Thanks to the charting, she noticed something else. The snakes were coming before an opportunity to get angry. They weren't punishment. They came to warn her so she could avoid the conflict. She felt God was trying to protect her body from further stress and harm.

The snakes became a helpful tool. If she woke with the sensation of having her head lay on the body of a snake (she could feel the pounding of his pulse), she was not surprised that an opportunity for a new problem came that day. She now saw them as challenges to be solved and herself as a problem solver.

Bugs were another unpleasant dream experience that turned into a helpful tool. She found bugs would come into her dreams about a week before a cold or flu knocked her down. She had time to prepare, time to get things done ahead, time to take off for a few days of recovery.

During one trying period, as the family gathered and prepared for her son's wedding, she dreamed of loosing two teeth. Picking them up she saw they both had delft blue paintings on them. This amused her because the family is Dutch. As the time progressed, both her mother-in-law and another son came down with a strong flu, one of them had to be rushed to emergency in the middle of the night.

Was there more help to be gotten from the night helpers?

Taking a clue from some of the books she was reading, she made lists in the back of her dream journal. She wrote a list of things she wanted to put into her life like a cure for arthritis, a better understanding of her life's goals, more money. She made another list of things she wanted out of her life, especially uncomfortable traits of her own like dandruff, hair falling out, feeling weak, grinding teeth, allowing people to manipulate her.

Vi paused in her writing. She'd not ground her teeth in her sleep for a long time now. She'd even gone to sleep without her mouth brace and not suffered from it. The list was working already!

One by one, she began crossing other things off the list. One of her wishes was to learn not to talk so much about herself.

The snakes would come when she was likely to do that. Talking about herself made her vulnerable. Letting people know too much about her seemed to bring trouble. She had yet to realize that natural instincts were trying to bubble up and change her life.

When her children were young, she used to write long letters to people, pouring out her every thought. She did it face to face, too. Again and again, these words came back to haunt her. Misunderstandings aside, she'd come to see that some extended family members pumped her for information and then turned it around to hurt her. Or, behind her back they'd twist her words and meanings. She was always left speechless when one of these incidents got back to her. Just when she should have defended herself, she didn't.

She later came to forgive these people. As the sin being committed was as much her own as it was theirs. The sin was that of gossip. You open the doors to demons. When you over-in-dulge in anything, demons can walk in.

For now, she put talking too much on her list. She set out to keep her thoughts to herself. One evening, she was asked to drive a potential new member for chorus to rehearsal. She had been warned in a dream of snakes about this evening so it was a long silent ride. Neither of them talked much. They had a great time at rehearsal and against her better judgment; she talked about herself on the way home.

That night, the snakes angered her. It was either for the drive and the talk on the way home or for something that was to happen the next day. Vi took it as punishment for talking about herself, about her dreams.

Already she regretted her words. She had no real feedback from the new lady to see if she enjoyed the conversation or thought Vi needed psychiatric help. That night Vi told the snakes, "I don't need you to punish me!"

Analyzing the situation, she realized that her fear of snakes did not protect her or warn her, as she'd come to believe. They failed to keep her from watching what she said. She reasoned that maybe she was looking at the message incorrectly. Dreams often mean the opposite of what they show. This is a perfect case to illustrate this point.

She had not yet learned to look at the action of a dream and then see all the possible meanings including the opposite action. She didn't know snakes held wisdom. Myths and science portray snakes as being on earth longer than man. By viewing man all this time, snakes hold centuries of wisdom ingrained as archetypes.

Also, the ability to go places people can't, brings the capacity to see things we don't see. It took Vi time to realize the snake was not only a messenger, but they also represented a part of her. As her animal instinct in her waking life began to build, the reptiles and animals grew bigger, more active until the time they took a different form.

Vi had wisdom trying to come out of the darkness of her unconscious. Her animal instinct, a piece of her personal puzzle she'd come into this world with, was an inner voice saying, "Believe in me!" Vi has a natural intelligence she'd been denying.

Today's dream workers call it a shadow of her personality because it was there all along, but she'd been repressing it. It was bubbling up in the archetypal form of snakes because it was time for this to be integrated into her ego, her public persona.

Often the things about ourselves we've repressed pop up in our dreams as pesky animals. Wild animals live by their natural instincts, something we humans forgot a long time ago. Think of the cave man or the early Indians use of dreams for everything. This has been pretty much universally repressed.

There may be a talent you could contribute to this world had you been further educated in it. Other times, when the instinct is known, but never integrated into our every day living, it shows up as something less wild with more human qualities, like Indians or small children.

Vi dreamed of providing blankets to Indians in her one room home. The bunks were over her head. She ran out of clean blankets and tried to use a dirty one, but the last Indian rejected it. The instincts she was using were about to run out of power. She was in over her head. By taking on so much, her blankets (her time) were now less than perfect and she had to cut back on what she was doing.

The struggle over the last clean blanket spoke of being an Indian Giver. By cutting back on some things she would feel like an Indian Giver, going back on promises. The dream was pointing out a better consideration of priorities.

What we think is right and what God has planned for us, can be very different things. Vi became a whole person, when she followed the bigger plan. Sometimes, as with Vi, life will take over and solve the problem. If she'd understood her dreams sooner, she may have had a much less painful, and quicker, resolution.

For Vi, more, rather than less, opportunity came for her to talk about her dreams. The snakes had come to shake her up, get her over her fear of talking about herself. The snakes were saying believe in yourself, come out of the cave of darkness, into the light of day. Vi realized this was good for God also. Like the earlier message where God said, "I make my money on reruns."

Vi relaxed with new relationships. She let the talk flow and found help coming through her words to people. While manning a table for the arthritis foundation, during a quiet spell a wonderful, elderly lady sat down and they began talking. The conversation turned to dreams and Vi wondered aloud why she was telling her these things.

The lady said, "There must be a reason, I'm interested in dreams too. I have a recurring dream that won't leave me alone." The woman actually egged Vi on in her talk on dreams instead of arthritis.

"Tell me your dream," Vi said, "How long you've had it and when was the last time?"

The lady patted her chest, remembering. "I wake in a sweat. A thief chases me. He wants my purse. That's all it is, but it scares me to death. I had it last night and it started a couple of years ago."

Vi thought for a minute and then advised her to go to sleep tonight, ask to see the chaser. "Make up your mind to turn around and give him your purse. Purses are really useless fashion statements. Men don't carry them. Another thing you might do is ask him what he wants of you."

"I can do that?" the lady asks.

"You can do it in a dream or in meditation," Vi went on, glad once again to have an audience. "The thief is a part of you. This part may be saying it's time to give something up. Give up this purse you feel is so important. You can do without it."

A look of astonishment came over the ladies face. "I know what I'm holding onto that I don't need. It's my independence. My son offered a couple of years ago to make a home for me attached to his home. He built it. I wouldn't have to worry about rent or utilities. I wouldn't be alone if I didn't want to be. Now that we've talked, I think that may be it. But is it telling me to move in or hold on?"

Vi didn't know, but made her usual offer. "If you want, I'll dream for you tonight and see what answer I get."

"That would be wonderful." The lady reached into her purse retrieving a pen and paper and wrote her name and address for Vi. "Here is my name and address and phone number."

Vi's dreams that night showed a moving truck being loaded. She wrote it out and mailed it to the lady. Within a week Vi received a letter from the lady's son thanking her for convincing his mother to make the move.

The material and encounters brought through via the snakes gave Vi lots of new experiences to talk about, some funny things. She even began to make jokes that made other people laugh. She suddenly realized that she liked herself. She was glad she took their advice and became more open.

The snakes disappeared except for the occasional warning of an opportunity for an argument to come. What she learned was that she really needed to let herself be herself and to love herself for who she is. She enjoyed sharing her experiences and helping others with her stories. God seemed to be bringing the people to her who needed to hear her experiences.

A phone call came asking Vi to talk on her experiences before a metaphysical church. Her friend Phyllis arranged a talk before a Community College Luncheon meeting.

So Vi began giving public speeches on dreams. The doubters didn't offend her. The benefits of people coming up afterwards, sharing their own dream stories and asking for dreams far outweighed any negatives.

You either send your demons away or make them allies. Working with dreams, you gain strength to overcome whatever negative patterns you see in your life. When you are afraid, you are squeezing God out of that portion of your life. With God you should fear nothing – not death, not demons. If you have fear, you don't have God! Vi was sure of this, it was in the Bible, but …

Any exchange with the neighbors still bothered her. She wondered why did it bother her so deeply? This was business. You can't please all of the people all of the time. Ray and Vi had a right to try to make the most money they could. "Anyone else owning this property would. Even if the guy across the street owned it. He'd make all kinds of changes in an attempt to make money. They would, why shouldn't I?" Vi thought.

She cried herself sick. She considered. "My neighbors had opposed me about a change to my business property. Why the great hurt? Was it losing my right to make some badly needed money? Was it being publicly humiliated when they stood in public hearings accusing me of a dirty kitchen, or saying they taped their phone calls to me and I was nasty, or was it having what I considered a brilliant idea shot down?"

She had slipped into meditation thinking on these things, why the hurt?

Thoughts of a friend she'd recently lost came to mind. Mary lived on another road. She, her husband, Ray and Vi spent many evenings together. Though both couples were busy, Mary called them often to come over. They had no boat, just lived along the lake and they really liked Ray and Vi. Ray and Vi liked them. They knew the other neighbors and were innocent bystanders in this war. Mary expressed feeling uncomfortable being in the middle, friends of both sides, so Vi let her go. She had not objected. Vi felt rejected. It hurt.

This was not a memory Vi dredged up. It came out of nowhere and so Vi knew it to be a message from God. Now she asked God, were there other times? Did she do something wrong?

He showed her more. Vi once more, in meditation, lived through an argument with her eighteen-year-old daughter that had left her sick. Then she lived through a family party where she'd come home and vomited. She'd thought she'd had food poisoning or was just sick. The truth was now before her. It was the situation that caused her reaction.

Hard as this was to do, Vi found it fascinating because the situations were shown in the order of their happening, going from now into the past chronologically. Sure this was leading to a great discovery, she vowed to continue as soon as she could get some more time.

The next day, she found time. She unplugged the phone, turned off the marine radio, and locked the doors. She sat in a chair with arms and a fairly straight back, closed her eyes and thought on what she'd seen yesterday. At first parts of a shopping list began to take form. She pushed it aside and asked why the hurt? Other things came and she pushed them aside. Finally she realized she'd been through a whole story and would not have been able to stop it if she wanted to. This was a message from God. She wrote it down. It was another time she'd gotten so angry and felt so powerless that she became ill.

After a few sessions of this, Vi was led to the scene of her parents announcing their divorce when she was eight. This surprised her. The two asked her to make a choice of which one of them she wanted to live with. Not wanting to hurt either of their feelings, she asked for her grandmother, her father's mother. Her older brother had lived with her in order to attend a special school and so she felt she could do this also.

She always knew the divorce had nothing to do with her personally, but then she remembered what she'd repressed. She couldn't remember seeing either of them after that, not for a long time. She knew this was rejection. Each of the other hurts had been a form of rejection.

"How had this shaped my life?" She wondered. "What had this to do with my neighbors hurting me? Could I have avoided all this hurt? Will I continue to have these problems?" There was a lot she didn't understand. Understanding is another step.

Her parents deserted her when she was young. To her knowledge, this had been a catalyst to do better with her life than they had done with theirs. There were things they did that Vi would not do. Smoking and drinking were two of them.

Vi always thought she'd made a good decision. She knew she'd made the best choice and never regretted the move, after looking at her parents separate lives from then on.

Gram and Grandpa were good, stable parents. What was there about this that made it an original hurt? What was she to do with this information now?

Each big hurt, including the hurt this fight with her neighbors, was somehow tied to this. Were other, future situations of rejection destined to be harmful to her health? She needed to turn this around, now.

Darlene walked into her life. She was an angel. An angel in the form of an acquaintance, God often uses other people to speak to us.

As they sat on some rocks by the beach, one sunny noontime,

Vi shared her path and her confusion. Darlene pointed out the amazing things Vi had accomplished on her own.

Since starting her dream study, wonderful spiritual things had happened. Among the good was her improving health and her ability to dream for others. She'd been helpful in saving a man lost on the lake.

She relied on her messages and had an appreciation of herself as a special person. God was talking to her.

Darlene pointed these things out and added that any child of her parents would have been treated the same way. They each had their own paths of life and lessons to learn. Actually, if they had not treated Vi as they did, she would not be the person she is today.

Since she had come to like herself, she had a lot to thank them for and prayed to be forgiven for the times that she'd treated her parents with less than love.

Darlene helped her see this. God was working through her to give Vi this message that she needed so much. Vi calls her an angel for this.

A message from God is not to be wasted. It was time to put her newfound knowledge to work. We always act on the messages to show our dedication, our sincerity. We must keep the messages flowing.

Back in mediation Vi asked, "What now?"

She found herself reliving each of those incidents. Issues arose one by one. The arguments with other kids, the issues with relatives as she grew older and finally about the neighbors and the marina.

This time she saw them with a different light. These people were each walking their own paths, suffering their own hurts. Vi saw herself over reacting. Forgiving these people was not even an issue. She asked God to forgive her for the way she had acted.

No one had to be actually confronted. Vi's attitude changed and old relationships got better for it. A great weight was lifted from her shoulders. That big heap of dung buried deep down inside was breaking up, floating away, making room for more good things.

Not all the relationships healed. The problems with the neighbors needed some intervention bigger than Vi had at her disposal. Then, sometimes, what we think is important and what God sees as important are two different things.

Chapter 7

Predicted Healing
November 1986

Ray and Vi spent Thanksgiving alone. Both children left in the area were married into large families and each had sat by Vi's table, eating very little because they were going to the in-laws. You get to pick your battles and this seemed a loosing one for Ray and Vi. Yet why sit by and feel sorry for yourself?

Vi asked Ray, "Do we have to stay here for Christmas and feel left out again?"

"What do you have in mind?" Ray asked with a curious look.

Vi replied with a smile, "Remember how my Dad and Step-mother always went to Bethlehem, PA, for Christmas? This was their tradition. Maybe we should make a tradition? Something we could look forward to."

"It would be fun taking a road trip, just the two of us. Why don't you look into it and see what you come up with?" Ray said.

Vi watched the travel ads, read the newspaper. In the most unlikely place, the County Pennysaver, she found a small classified ad for the rental of a condo in Myrtle Beach. The price was right. It would be only one night on the road to drive there. So they made arrangements to rent it for the two weeks including Christmas and New Years. On the way home they could even stop in Virginia Beach and visit the A.R.E. buildings where Edgar Cayce things were kept. She was looking forward to visiting A.R.E.

The dreams at this time were interesting.

Ray and Vi were operating a second marina for the next county. Here a politician named Riley was the person they answered to. He answered to the voters. Ray and Vi put their daughter and new husband in a small cottage on the property for round the clock security presence and help with the work.

Being a large municipal marina near a large city, many interesting people crossed their path. Because politician Riley wanted to please everybody, he often made mountains out of molehills to get his name in the paper. All in all, it was a good relationship. Nothing ever runs smoothly.

One dream Vi had was about Mr. Riley retiring and moving to a new home he was having built on the lake. Thinking this extremely funny, whether it was a prediction or not, it was fun to imagine. Vi told a few close friends and relatives.

Another dream that stayed with her, was of a friend of theirs named LeRoy playing the piano. She had never known him to have that talent in real life, but in the dream she kept telling him how beautiful his music was. She kept saying, "LeRoy, LeRoy, LeRoy," over and over again.

Another dream that she recognized could be about Myrtle Beach, was a scene of horses being unloaded from barges in a canal next to the beach. Vi, in the dream, laughed about having paid all this money to dodge horse plops when they walked the beach.

Writing her dreams was just something she did, religiously. Even if she didn't understand them, she gave each one a title, and built a table of contents as she went along. This helped to find the dream if it turned out to be a prediction.

She received many predictions. A couple weeks before, she'd seen an upheaval in an office, papers flying all over the place. She shared it the next day over breakfast. Her thoughts were either a stock market crash, a huge snowstorm or the US would go to war. All three happened within the next week. It was a good time to get somewhere warmer.

Her focus was not on the predictions, but they added some spice to her study. She told Ray they were given to maintain her interest and to remind her someone other than herself was talking to her in the dreams.

As they drove into the city of Myrtle Beach, Vi began seeing things she had recorded in her dream book. The first things she noticed were huge elephants and giraffes in a miniature golf course they drove around.

Then the entrance signs to the condo complex said LeRoy Springs. Remember the LeRoy dream?

As they pulled up to the building, another foreseen image waited for them. A van was unloading horses to be ridden on the beach. There it was and, yes, they were worried about horse droppings.

Inside the condo they heard another dream image. The planes roared over their heads heading out to sea and were just like another dream recorded in Vi's book. By now she had the book out, checking up on all these coincidences or synchronicities as Jung would call them. An airbase was situated right behind the condo. Thank goodness they only flew during the day. It was a novelty to watch them.

Ray and Vi went out and picked up a newspaper to check out local events. The front-page headline hit her. There, on the front page of Myrtle Beach's newspaper, the governor, by the name of Riley, was retiring to a home he had built on a lake.

These were too many things to be just coincidences. Somewhere there had to be a message for Vi. Edgar Cayce said nothing ever happens by chance. That night she laid her pad and pencil on the table next to the bed and went to sleep. The nightmare she had that night was terrible.

She dreamed she was singing with the Sweet Adeline's, but no matter how hard she tried, she couldn't get it right. She couldn't hear herself. The other singers thought Vi was terrible. They realized something was wrong and felt sorry for her. The sympathy was worse than punishment. Vi woke up sobbing.

She sat up the rest of the night, afraid she'd return to the dream if she went back to sleep. She was convinced God wanted her to make one more change. The next morning she talked it out with Ray. The only thing they could think to change was to throw her pills away. It would be better to live with pain than to loose her hearing or her sanity like the dream suggested. They threw them away. They talked about how lucky they were to live in a ranch house, no stair climbing. They'd just scale back their expectations in life.

Vi and Ray knew they'd been brought here to Myrtle Beach to learn something. Unless something else happened, this was it.

They enjoyed Myrtle Beach as best they could. The pain really wasn't bad. The swellings would get bad, but then ice packs would take them down. Later, Vi was to learn that an overdose of aspirin, the pill she was on, would cause a ringing in the ear. This would explain the image in the dream of singing the wrong way, because she couldn't hear herself sing. Ringing in the ear or loss of hearing was to be feared. She didn't have the information to make that connection, at the time of the dream.

Two weeks later, she went back to the doctor for more blood tests. There was no arthritis in her blood stream. Now she realizes a tingling in her joints is her signal to step back from life, and take things easier until it blows over again. It works. It's been working for 19 years.

Chapter 8

2004

Ray and Vi relaxed over lemonade in the Florida Room of their new home in Florida. A soft breeze blew in the open windows that gave a view of the back yard Vi had seen in a dream the night before they first saw the house. The yard between their house and the one in back of theirs was common land. A commercial firm mowed the area and wood poles with power lines to the houses ran down the middle.

Usually, when looking for a place to live, Vi and Ray have always stayed away from power lines. In her dream, Vi saw a community of small, similar houses all in a row, like was popular in the sixties. Common ground separated the back yards where the lines ran. In the dream, Vi saw herself swimming underground, laying more power lines.

She took this as a sign that this community they'd decided on was to be a good place for them. She would be laying her own power lines, her life's work. When she walked out that back door with the realtor and saw the exact vision of her dream, she had no qualms about taking this place. It was many small homes all alike, exactly like the dream.

They still marveled at the vision and now talked of a few things, like a dishwasher, that the vision did not contain. "That'll come," Ray told Vi. He'd started a handy man business of his own and was having a great time being everyones hero, being able to fix the things they couldn't. He'd gathered a lot of practical knowledge over the years.

"Does your dream group meet tonight?" Ray asked.

"No, we switched to Saturday mornings," Vi replied.

Ray smiled, "Great! I found a new restaurant today. I want to take you to it for supper." He paused, then asked, "Did you ever think we'd be so contented?"

Vi replied, "It was meant to be. We're finally doing what God wanted of us. I wish I'd understood the dream messages better, and sooner, maybe I'd not have had to go through the hurts and embarrassments. Maybe, if we'd moved to Florida sooner, I'd not have slipped on the ice and broken my leg."

"If you're going to think that way," Ray said, "maybe we'd not have lost so much money in our flower shop. But, who'd have known?"

"I should have," Vi replied, "if I understood my dream messages and other signs."

"I have to say I enjoyed the last three years managing the RV Park, even though it came to a bad ending," Ray said.

"It was time to move on." Vi said. "I'll never forget that dream I had the first night I was in North Carolina at dream school." Vi had seen a dream course advertised in the Dream Network Magazine. She was browsing through, admiring her own article and photo when the ad for the Haden Institute Dream Study Group Leadership Course caught her eye. She'd signed up immediately.

It required three intensive weekends in North Carolina the first year. Her first night there, being nervous about committing the money, making the trip by herself and just being among strange people, she'd had what she thought was a compensating dream. When your life goes too far in one direction, your dream will give you an experience to bring balance. Vi had woken up from this dream laughing. Just the relief her mind and body needed, she thought.

The students in her group chose her dream to analyze. Laughter was not always good, they said. It often is mocking. In the dream, Dick and George, two men from the RV Park who helped out a lot, were on an old-fashioned railroad work cart that is powered by two people pushing up and down on a center pole arrangement to power the cart along the tracks. Vi watched from the edge of a laughing crowd as they used this method to paint a yellow stripe down the center of the road. The funniest part was that, unbeknownst to George, Dick was also putting the yellow paint all over George.

The dream students felt the dream was a foretelling of something bad. It was work related. Vi acknowledged this was possible, but held to her first impression until she got home and the next day the bosses came and let them go. They were the 24th managers in a 25-year history. And their immediate boss also got fired. This was a shock, but the divineness of it struck home when, traveling to the post office to change their address, they noticed a county road crew was painting yellow stripes down the center of the road.

Now, settled in a retirement community, Vi was in her element. She had dream school and dream groups underway. She was writing about dreams and emailing people across the country as a result of her on-going articles in the magazine.

Vi said, "You know, I've only had two incidents where I felt the arthritis try to creep back into my joints. One was right after getting fired! I dropped everything and concentrated on healing with meditation. I visualize the white light of God surrounding me and going through me. I see myself floating on the top of a cloud, feeling safe and secure. A few days of that and the pains disappeared."

"The pace of life can bring any disease out of its hiding place," Ray agreed.

At age 65, Vi has one enlarged knuckle, but no other signs of arthritis. She did develop the diabetes, but is able to control that with diet alone. An accident (or was it a message from God?), which resulted in a broken leg and three operations on the leg, led her to this warmer climate where she had less pain and was able to progress with her dream work. In this new living area, dream work is much more accepted and fruitful. Many new opportunities opened up for her dream work that weren't in New York State.

"Do you still like the dream course?" Ray asked. "Don't you go again next month?"

"Yes, yes." Vi quickly replied. "I've met several authors and dream researchers. Jeremy Taylor, the author of *Where People Fly and Water Runs Upstream* and several others are there almost every time. Bob Hoss, Executive Director of the International Society for the Study Of Dreams was our main teacher last time. It's exciting."

After starting the dream course she formed two dream study groups, studied a lot of writings by and about noted psychologist Carl G. Jung and began meeting many leading dream researchers.

Vi went on, "All these years, eighteen now since I began this dream study, I've done a lot of dreams for other people. But never understood the interpretations or why or how it all happened. Jung must have had much of the same experiences I did. I'm glad he had the resources to dig as deep as he did for answers for us."

"Are you still dreaming for others?" Ray asked.

"Yes," Vi said, "But I'm limited physically. If there were a demand for my special skill, three a week would be my limit. I need time for my own dreams. Now I'm helping many more people by teaching them to understand their own dreams."

Ray asked, "Are people in your groups able to catch their dreams and gain understanding?"

Vi eagerly replied, "There've been some personal breakthroughs for some of them"

"How?" Ray wanted to know.

"The dreams point out what they should be worrying about," Vi said. "They learn how to feel about it, what is not important. Dreams guard their health, their emotions, their vocations, and their relationships. Dreams point the way to living the best life they can, one step at a time."

"Sounds like a long journey," Ray said, "I suppose people have more than one issue to solve."

"We push along, sometimes learn our lessons – sometimes not. Carl Jung called this journey, if we do it right, 'individuation.'" Vi went on. "It means a psychic development that leads to the conscious awareness of being whole. I followed the messages in my dreams, changed a lot of things, some opportunities walked in and, hopefully, I'm now what they consider whole (whoever 'they' might be). I hope there's no more big lessons to learn."

"I'm whole without all this," Ray joked.

"That could be your ego speaking," Vi said, "It blocks one's growth sometimes, but you look okay to me, too."

"I still have a dream once and a while," Ray said.

"Yes, and you still come to me to find out what they mean," Vi replied. Something popped into her mind. "We're not supposed to see into the future, you know. Things aren't set in concrete for us. We still make our own choices, just better ones once you tune into your dreams – and you are."

Looking back, it was easy for Vi to see Jung's theory of individuation at work in her own life. Several of Jung's terms struck familiar chords with Vi. One was the word "Animus." Before 1985, many of her problems were the result of her animus at work.

"What was that big word you've been using, anumalis?" Ray asked.

"Either anima or animus," Vi answered, laughing. "You're reading my mind again. I was just thinking about that. It's the term Jung used for the dream figure who sometimes seems to be one's helper or it may lead us into bad places, for the greater good. Jung said this is our connection with our inner or higher self. I think he means God. It's that person or being deep down inside us that knows us better than we do, and wants what's best for us."

Vi continued, "I know it's the helper or adjuster in my life. When I see a person of the opposite sex in my dreams, it's a representative of my inner self. This self is deep in the unconscious regions, so deep within people don't know it's there, except when we see it in dreams. If we're intuitive or maybe have been doing self-searching, we can find it in the things that happen around and to us in life."

"Is that the person who looks through my eyes when I pass a mirror and thinks, so that's what other people see?" Ray asked.

"Sometimes," Vi replied. "There's a story in Greek mythology that might explain it better. The story has it that men and women were once born into one big body. It had four arms, four legs and a two-sided head. This human was tremendously intelligent, happy, and complete in every way. The Gods, being jealous, split them in half. Now we spend our earthly lifetimes searching for our soul mate, our other half. I found my other half inside me. That's where I found clues to loving myself, to being complete, by myself. I was amazed to read Jung knew about this being too and this place inside also. He called it one's unconscious memory."

"You mean I'm not your soul mate?" Ray asked.

"No, you just remind me of him," Vi said.

"So, is my other side a guy or a girl?" Ray asked.

"A man looks for the perfect female or anima. People are always looking for that perfect someone to make them feel complete – but it's not a person," Vi said.

"Do we have to dream to find this?" Ray was really into this.

"No," Vi said, "If we are wise enough, we can see this opposite side of ourselves in our projections. Waking or sleeping, our unconscious knows his/her other half and projects this image, of what we need to make us whole onto other people. Women, for instance, before becoming whole, project their longings onto various males. This in itself can cause problems in a woman's life. Then to, this explains why, after being together a while, the polish or projection sometimes wears off the friend we've chosen. Women finally see him for himself, not who we want him to be."

"Well, you women don't always measure up after a while either. Any head of cabbage stinks after a while," Ray said.

"Except us," Vi replied.

"Yeah, except us," Ray agreed.

"Theory has it," Vi continued, "that a man expects to find what he sees of his anima, the parts missing in himself, in a real life woman. He doesn't realize it's something another person can't give him. He admires it and wants to make it his own. It's already in him; he just hasn't realized it yet."

After some thought she added, "I'll take watching on my dreams any day. We get clues as to what we might project before we do it. It might save us from looking for something in another person until we have it firmly within ourselves. The time is worth the effort when you consider you might avoid life knocking you down."

"Relationships aren't the only things that cause problems in life," Ray says.

"You're right," Vi agreed. "The qualities of this other half pertain to other things as well. We have this longing for something different in our lives from romance to work to just something better – the grass is always greener syndrome. It also comes from deep inside our unconscious. It's a feeling of being unfulfilled or of needing something, but we don't know what. I've seen times in my life and others lives of projecting that longing onto others in surprising ways. Jealousy, hate, envy, love, and hero worship are among some of the strong emotions we can have that we sometimes aren't even aware we have. "

"In my own childhood," Vi continued, "I experienced rejection, abandonment, looking for someone to take care of me, but I also had talents I didn't know I had. These are other objects of projection. I see them in others and it brings a physical reaction in me. We knew these things onetime, but we repressed them."

She went on, "It could be a way of behaving. It could be

something someone is ashamed of. What if a parent told you not to talk so much, not to make up stories, yet being a storyteller is part of who you were meant to be? You try to please your parent so this part of who you are gets buried deep in your personal unconscious and erupts years later, often as nightmares. When you do begin to realize there are other parts to your personality you'd like to explore, you might develop emotional problems like guilt or self-loathing for living out a natural tendency because you were once told it is not acceptable. Yet, while it's repressed, it can make you physically ill."

"That's what happened to you," Ray said.

"Yes," Vi agreed. "With dream work I finally gave in, integrated it into who I was and I wondered why I'd waited so long. It opened doors of opportunities and brought a happiness I'd never thought possible. I had to learn to be the writer, the photographer, and the singer, to help me heal. I also had to learn to like myself, recognize my strengths and give up my shyness, talk so others could benefit from what I've learned."

"What were some of your projections?" Ray wondered.

"The things I repressed that I projected onto others?" Vi asked. Ray nodded.

"Let me see," Vi said, "Okay. I'd form attachments and would be devastated when these people did not live up to the qualities I put on them. I depended on others too much. My own sense of worthiness had to fight its way up to be part of my public personality or persona. I projected a dislike onto anyone who was comfortable in his or her skin. They might have been an inspiration for me had I not turned my back on them. Remember how I tried to reject you?"

"You and your grandmother did a fine job of that," Ray reminisced. "I'd arrive every night at 7 PM and you both did all you could to discourage me."

"Well, you were like clockwork. You left at 10 PM and never said a word. How strange is that?" Vi rolled her eyes.

"I didn't speak the language," Ray defended himself, "That's how I learned; listening to you two talk about me, wondering if I'd ever leave. You didn't get away with it. I was sure what I wanted."

"Well," Vi said, "As a teenager, this was the only chance at rebellion I had. I was tossed by circumstances from the beginning. As a teenager I was trying to make my own choices. You seem to be one more person choosing for me."

Ray grinned. He came from Holland, when they were both 17; he fixed his sure-of-himself, Aries, eye on her and claimed her for life.

Vi talked on, "Although I wasn't aware of anything like this anima/animus theory, I had daydreams of you as a child. My daydreams were always the same story, owning a ranch complete with singing cowboys, horses, cattle, etc. After beginning my spiritual experience, I recognized you as the ranch foreman who was always there to help me when I needed help. The cattle roundup and responsibilities became the boats in our marina, the way we protected them and worked together."

Vi continued, "I found out about this animus thing on my own, but I didn't know its name or theory until I studied Jung. Early in my dream study, in 1985-1986, I thought the figure of you was you. If, in a dream, you slept while I worked, I thought it an exaggeration of what I experienced during the day. Sorry if I tended to find fault with you back then.

"Then you, or the 'Ray' in my dreams changed. At first I'd dream of tending children, fixing supper, answering the door, etc. and this 'Ray' figure slept. Good thing I never attempted to change you, or anyone else. As time passed, the dreams changed."

She went on, "My attitudes towards life and other people and situations changed, as I grew, 'you' one day became a moving, speaking part of my dreams again. Your life hadn't changed, just the 'you' in my dreams. This was a big change and I knew it signified something special had changed for me. I knew I was on the right track when I saw that the 'Ray' of my dreams and I were once more becoming one. We were working together."

"Come on. You still get angry sometimes," Ray couldn't wait to get this in.

"Not as much," Vi said, "I see situations that I might be inclined to get embroiled in while writing my dreams. After living through the dream, they're not important to me anymore."

Ray challenged, "If you dreamed of my mother driving into the driveway, I bet you'd get upset before it actually happened. You'd be mad the rest of the day"

Vi laughed, "More likely the dream would have me being attacked by a mother lion. That's a symbol and an exaggeration. Now

I'd laugh when I figured out this meant your mother was coming. I automatically reject the situation; refuse to get bothered by it. I might suddenly find a need to go shopping for the day."

She added, "In the course of a day's work or normal relationships, I still have knee-jerk reactions to some things. With most of the usual old problems I'm now wise enough to wonder why did that ever bother me?"

"Big change!" Ray said.

"Because of my dreams," Vi went on, "I have the potential to do better with my life and I want to help others find that in themselves. Feelings of hate, envy, love, hero worship can point to the potential that is alive and well in us, but unless we work with our dreams we don't see this side. It's a very real energy coming up from our unconscious."

"What have I repressed?" Ray asked.

"I haven't a clue," Vi thought a minute. "Being an Aries, maybe, gives you a sureness of being right, you don't hesitate to say what you think, and never get in trouble for it. There are things we bring into this world and have never taken the time to develop. That was part of my problem. I came into this world to be and do certain things. Those things got buried and they had to fight to get out. I don't know anyone else who's worked on this. Most people around me never seem to recognize this, never reach for their potential."

"You're not talking about me?" Ray asked.

"No," Vi said, "I'm talking about people who don't want to hear about it. They never think of such things."

"What would a new beginning look like in a dream?" Ray asked.

Vi gathered her thoughts and said, "There are a few things, a death makes way for a new beginning. A baby being born or children in my dreams, usually some I don't even know, would come when something formerly repressed decides it's time to grow. Our own children at younger ages could represent a part of me that is growing. It's not exactly a new beginning when they are passed the baby stage, but definitely something we've forgotten about. If you saw an egg or a new plant sprouting, that would signify a new beginning, or turning a corner"

Vi went on, "Working with my dreams helped a lot. I caught a glimpse of the buried parts of myself trying to surface and often waited on making any decisions. I had a way different attitude because I'd seen the potential of a similar new thing in my dreams."

Before she began following her dreams, these energies erupted in waking life and they caused all kinds of havoc. Her dream study was a lonely path, but it led to her life's purpose, inner realization of her talents, who she was meant to be, and appreciation of herself. Now she had the time and resource to help others find their gold.

"You know," Vi said, "we all are born with the ability to dream. That's something no one can take away. Before capturing my dreams I spent years not owning anything or loosing what I had. It seemed every good thing or idea was taken over by others. Now I have something no one can take away and I'm extremely confident and happy being me."

"Was there a turning point to realizing you were happy with yourself?" Ray asked.

Vi nodded enthusiastically, "The day I found my ability to make people laugh. It was a few days, actually. The first couple of times people laughed at what I said, I was stunned. Then it happened at an Arthritis Support Group meeting. Something I said had everyone sharing a laugh. At that moment I realized I liked myself. The feeling never left."

Ray wondered, "You feel an authority over yourself, like finally in control of your actions?"

Vi replied, "I feel I've gone beyond a stage of childhood. Children need authority, guidance and laws. When I grew up a little, I came to realize there are all kinds of authority, guidance and laws from the realm of dreams, from the realm of the collective unconscious. That's what guides me now."

Ray shifted back a topic or two. "We were talking about theme shifts. Were there any others like me sleeping and then waking up?"

Vi nodded yes and said, "Other major shifts in my dreams happened. I followed the themes of my dreams as well as the symbols. Themes reflect the major issues going on in my life. The symbols are expressions of my personal characteristics, attitudes, and behaviors. The shift in themes helped me chart my personal growth. That's a thing nice to know.

"There was a period where you and I, in my dreams, were

always helping other people run their businesses. I think this precluded our RV Park management years," Vi continued, "Then another major shift came in a dream where I was asked to drive two boats to their home docks by two different men. One boat was small, the other large. I agreed, but when I arrived at each dock, the reception was the same. Neither man intended to pay me and each time, in the dream, I stood my ground and demanded payment and a ride home. Coming from someone who tried real hard to please everyone, this signaled a major step forward for me. My attitude about what I deserve out of life has changed. I feel real good about this dream."

"Has anyone in your group reported a change like that?" Ray asked.

"Sonya, a lady in one of my dream groups, always had small children in her dreams," Vi eagerly told, "We tried using the symbol system to interpret them and 'if it were my dream.' The children would be small aspects of oneself, waiting to grow up. We asked questions like, 'What happened when you were five? What happened to you five years ago?' She always rejected these hypotheses. Recently she went to work at an elementary school. She laughs, now, about how hard she fought that school being built across the street from her home. Now she volunteers in the Kindergarten, tutors a couple of children and helps with special presentations.

"The great change in her dreams of children is that the images of children came to a stop. The theme was pointing out what she was to be doing with her life in order to be whole. Now I look for themes in the dreams of all the people in my groups."

"What's your reward for continuing this work? What do you expect to get out of it?" Ray asked.

This was an easy question for Vi. She said, "I've already gotten a lot. I can see where some people might say that's enough. I've become true to who I was meant to be with my writing, photographing, singing and dream work especially. My big reward for following the advise of my dreams is the opportunity to help others by dreaming for them. It has always convinced the other person that there is a God, Creator, Higher Intelligence, whatever they believe. It often gave straight out answers to their questions and always opened their minds to greater possibilities.

"Jung had a theory that people experiencing individuation often came to a point in life where they adopt a Jesus complex, a feeling of having the special powers of God. It would have been easy to get carried away with this gift, but I never did. This dreaming for others may be considered my Jesus complex except I never believed it to be a special gift of mine alone. My constant push has been for other people to do the same.

"Besides, each time I have an inclination of greatness, God, Spirit, whomever shoots me down. One more of Mom's old sayings, 'God has ways of making you humble'."

"Humble is good," Ray said.

Vi agreed, "I remembered the verse in the Bible in Matthew 19:14 – 'Let the little children come to me.' It took on new meaning. I felt I had become humble like a child, non-judging, curious to learn. That's true humbleness."

"Did this memory come in dreams?" Ray asked.

"Oh yeah!" Vi replied, "Woke up with it on my mind. Then another time I had a lot of busy little mice in my dreams. Humble as a church mouse and poor as a church mouse came to mind. Maybe that's why they were there; slowing down my expectations or any feelings I might have had of greatness. I never lost sight of the fact that the messages did not come from me. I never knew what answers I'd get when asking for a dream for somebody. I have a two-way communication with a higher power. It's help is worth the time."

Ray thought about it and said, "I believe." He tried to clear up his position and continued, "I just don't talk about it. It's personal. I think about it sometimes. When I'm driving on the highway I see my father in the shape of the clouds or a car goes by and I swear your grandmother is in the front passenger seat."

"Spirituality comes in different degrees, levels of acceptance. I'm a searcher," Vi said. "Why, when, how. I'll fill you in on what I find out and you can take or leave it."

"That's a deal," Ray said.

Chapter 9

Religion After Dream Study

A few weeks later, Ray was ready to hear more about Vi's quest for knowledge of spirituality. He asked, "Did this dream experience change what you learned in church as a child?"

Vi replied, often hesitating as she gathered her thoughts, "It opened many doors of understanding. I came to read the Bible passages differently. I sometimes read them like one of my dreams and I find new ways of interpreting them, different than what I'd grown up with. The stories, the parables have so many different meanings now. I found answers that satisfied me, but other people wouldn't believe me. That left me with more questions. I needed to find out exactly what had happened to me during my first two years of spiritual work in 1985 and 1986. The 'how' of the story, how all the changes and miracles came to me became clear after reading Jung and his science of psychology." She hesitated, "Although I was thrilled to find Jung, when I first delved into his writings, I didn't see anything spiritual. I believed Jung, but I wouldn't give up on God.

"Just a day or two before reading *Man and His Symbols* written by Jung, Von Franz, Henderson, Jacobi and Jaffe," Vi continued. "I recorded a dream where I was confronted by a man who'd turned a dog into a partially mechanical being. I knew I had to kill this man and bury the dog deep in the ground. Then, reading the book, I came across the word 'mechanical' several times. Jung had written, 'The interpretation of dreams cannot be turned into a mechanical system and then crammed into unimaginative minds.'"

"Maybe there was a spiritual side to Jung," Ray said.

Vi replied, "Yes, as far as my beliefs go, I knew my dreams were directing me to hold on to the spiritual. I knew I was getting help from deep inside myself, even from a source beyond myself. Those dreams were anything, but mechanical."

Ray jumped in, "Turn the dog (the message) back into a flesh and bone, heart beating dog. Underground would be deep in the unconscious, where one would expect to find the message."

"You're listening!" Vi exclaimed, "Some of the dream messages I've experienced have surprised me. They're not things that I'd read about in any books. These things required an open mind. All by yourself, it's hard to know 'believe or not believe,' but God seems to bring me who and what I need at just the right time to convince me. Since I'd had my wake up call (so to speak) I've found many more people also traveling this path, having these miracles and spiritual experiences. I've also witnessed organized religion incorporating some things previously left to the mystics into their services, things like meditation, the word 'spirituality', some are acknowledging an inner source for 'God' rather than a figure out there on a throne. I read a lot of signboards in front of churches and I read a lot of church ads."

"Yeah, I noticed!" Ray laughed.

Vi continued, "Since attending the Haden Institute I've met ministers who were searching for a personal experience with God through dreams and self-introspection. At weekend intensives in North Carolina I've met Methodist ministers, Presbyterian ministers, Catholic leaders and others from all over the U.S. also studying the subject. There's hope that some of society's doors are opening that were not open before."

"What will be the benefit of the church adopting this idea?" Ray asked.

"I think," Vi replied, "If dream work and acceptance of a personal relationship with one's creator was adopted by organized religion, the world would have a better chance. Just think of the networks of millions of people that can be reached in a short time. I assume God is working on the other side making these people ready to hear this.

"At one weekend Dream Intensive the main speaker was Robert Hoss, Past President of the International Association for The Study of Dreams. He'd just returned from a meeting of that group in Switzerland. He said there were twenty countries represented and 120 papers presented on dream research."

"Twenty countries where people study dreams? Amazing," Ray said, "So, was Jung scientific?'

Vi said, "Jung used scientific jargon and packed his experience and knowledge in the box of science. He's quoted, as saying he hoped others would continue his quest for truth. My big want is to be one of those who continue his work and have a chance to share what I've learned."

Vi thought back to her beginnings. Brought up in a Dutch Reformed Church, Gram took her there for Sunday Service, Sunday school, choir, and to be at her side for women's groups. They studied the Bible and Vi absorbed more than she thought she did. Her Gram also dragged her to Lake Ave. Baptist Church to a regular weekly women's sewing circle.

From time to time, when the situation merited, Vi made a few bargains with God. 'If you don't let Gram find out I ---, I will ----.' She believed in God because the adults around her said to. When she had children of her own to raise, she became active in church because it was the thing to do. She wanted to do what was right. Ray, the children and Vi attended a Methodist Church. Vi really got involved. She taught Sunday school from kindergarten thru high school, led youth group, sang in the choir, was a certified Lay Speaker and did many Sunday services including the sermon. She used to believe in God because that was the way she was brought up. She brought her children up the same way, but she didn't really know God.

"You know, Ray," Vi said, "When I got sick and began studying my dreams, that's when I came to KNOW God. I knew someone greater than me was talking to me. Edgar Cayce had said he always asked for the highest spirit to come through in his trances. Before I went to sleep, I did the same. It reminded me of the prayers my parents wanted me to say before bedtime. The results were astounding!

"I'd write a dream and the same words were repeated to me during that day from someone's talk and/or from a book I was reading and I knew I'd had a message from God.

"During one of my low spots, being desperate for a reason for living, I went into meditation and had visions of my talents. I knew it was from God. They weren't any talents I would have chosen.

"When needing to understand where I went wrong, I went into meditation. First my mind went to a shopping list. I dismissed it and tried again. Thoughts of something that happened yesterday came. I dismissed it and tried again. Suddenly I realized a whole story had gone through my head that I could not have stopped had I wanted to. I knew it was the voice of God.

"When people tried to put doubts into my head as to whether this was good or evil I remembered reading 1Timothy 4:4 where it says, 'For everything God created is good and nothing is to be rejected if it is received with thanksgiving because it is consecrated by the word of God and prayer.' (NIV Study Bible) Mt. 11:15 'He that hath ears to hear, let him hear.' King James Version. You know? I was hearing and it was good."

The revelations shown her were good because ultimately they led to a physical healing, a change of vocation and a change in attitude, which healed a lot of relationships including her relationship with herself.

She went on telling Ray, "In Genesis we're told the progression of the seven days it took God to create the earth. On the seventh day He rested. My church experience gave this as indication one should attend church once every seven days (Sundays). Since meditation was so helpful, my mind now translated this to a seventh of each day should be spent communing with God. A natural progression has been to be aware of God and open to His messages all the time. Perhaps one-seventh of my consciousness is tuned in this direction. I watch for meaningful synchronicities. I always acknowledge them by saying, thank you."

"Is the Unity Church you go to any different than the Methodist?" Ray wanted to know.

Vi said, "I feel at home at Unity. I'm not the only one studying dreams. I can learn from them. It's considered a Christian Metaphysical Church. They talk about God, Jesus and the Bible. It doesn't offer the sacrament of bread and wine. Those coming from traditional churches often miss the tradition until they realize the sacrament is all about communing with God, inviting Him into your consciousness. Unity people do that each week in their meditation time. I object in a way because they go into meditation, in church, and someone speaks wonderful words throughout. But we are not given the time to hear God's words. To me, this is what it's all about. People need to learn to hear the words of God for themselves. Through meditation and dream work, this can actually happen.

"There is another way to use meditation I found that's led me to have a better understanding of the Bible. When puzzling over a passage, I put my hand on the words I've just read and close my eyes in meditation. A whole new story comes to me. I get a view of the scene behind the scene. I get a clearer understanding."

"Like what?" Ray asked.

Vi replied, "I tried this with the words Jesus told His disciples. Asking them to follow Him, He said to leave everyone behind. One asked, 'What if my father were dying?' Jesus said, 'Let the dead bury the dead.' Now I know, the dead He referred to are the walking dead. They are the people dead to belief in God. Christian took on a different meaning for me that day."

"How about repentance?" Ray asked.

Vi laughed, "I've got a new meaning for the word 'repentance' also. For instance, when I dreamed of a time, as a child of twelve, being forced to eat a calf I'd raised and named. The lesson was, at 45, not to eat red meat. This is a change in consciousness. I no longer wanted beef. I wasn't sorry for eating it as repentance might suggest. My attitude change was that I no longer wanted it. Repentance is, 'never wanting to walk down that road again.' Remember the story of how St. Peter will quiz you at the pearly gates of Heaven on what you did or did not do?" Vi asked Ray, "How nice it would be for as many of us who can, to shorten that process for the Gatekeeper. I think working with our dreams will do that. I'm prepared to take my place as one of God's ready helpers."

"You've seen what Heaven is like?" Ray asked.

Vi relied, "Sure, the administration of Heaven is made up of committees. In my dreams I've visited the committee that works with people to get them to look within themselves. They work hard to send us messages, but if we won't listen, if a disaster is needed, they give it. That's tough love.

"I've seen the committee preparing souls to return to earth. The Gatekeeper there is an interesting, wise old man, dressed all in white with a long white beard.

"Another committee I've seen in my dreams is the prayer answering committee. In that dream a group of nuns sat around a big table taking the requests, one by one, and answered them based on the laws God has in place. God floated around behind them, peeking over their shoulders and occasionally changed a decision, granted a different outcome. I'm thinking that's 'Grace.'"

"What about all that time, between 1987 and 2000, you wrote plays?" Ray changed the subject.

Vi thought back, "My days of audience participation comedies that were murder mysteries. I wrote five plays and had six productions. You know, I wondered why writing murder mysteries was a talent I was led to pursue. This truly took (developed) a devious mind. I got an answer for that. It came in a dream where I was shown my own Heavenly future as being on the committee that gave people their dreams. Just think of the devious mind that it must take to come up with the story that can touch one's emotions and change a life. I'd have to know how they would feel about things, the things that can go wrong. Now I know why my life, before dream study, had been the way it was.

Chapter 10

Reincarnation Evidence

In 2005, Vi and I sat down to talk about some of her views and how she'd come to have them. I asked her to talk some more about one's life after death.

Vi said, "I've had scenes of life after death activities of myself and others. A man who was to design the 9th hole on a Heavenly golf course was shown to me just before he died. I didn't ask for the dream. The man is a close relative of mine and the dream story just seemed all about him. It was very straightforward. His father came, in the dream, and told me he was building him a mansion in a golfing community with all the great golfers. He said Arnold Palmer had just arrived. This coincided with Palmers' death. Father was a mason by trade so building a home makes sense. Telling my relative of this dream gave him something to anticipate that was pleasant. It gave him a chuckle and I hope some peace as he approached death"

"Kind of like the few times I was going under from anesthesia, I tried to think of something pleasant," I said.

"That's right," Vi said, "but looking forward to where you're going has got to take a lot of the fear out of dying."

"Do you think it got him through the gate any faster?" I asked.

"While not a humble person, he was sick for a long time and that brings on humbleness. Ray and I noticed a big change in his attitude about things during this time. Maybe he needed this sick time to clear up some baggage. I really can't say," Vi said.

"Vi, what about Jesus?" I asked. "Is He real? Will there be a second coming?"

Vi replied, "For non-Christians one must look to the office Jesus held as the Christ. Other religions have similar posts with different names. As a dream symbol, they mean the same. In Metaphysics and dream symbology, Jesus (other than the historical man) is a symbol for the possibility within each of us. Like the birth of a child in dreams, dream deaths, the child growing up can all refer to Him and the potential for good in each of us, the resurrection of a better me. The on-going dream story or theme with this child in different stages of life can mirror our own emotional growth, can go back and forth in age depending on what the outer situation is, and life in general can change if we apply what we see.

"My view is that Jesus is here now, working in each one of us who will listen. This is the second coming. He's stirring up the archetypes. I used to marvel at the increase in reported spiritual experiences in the world until I figured this out."

I had to ask, "How about good and evil?"

"God uses both," Vi said, "If you're a good parent, you allow your children to face challenges. God puts challenges in the way of his children to teach them. Look at the challenges He had to put in my way to get me to move to Florida where I could better pursue the dream work."

I nodded in agreement.

Vi continued, "Take nightmares. If someone walks ahead of you and you call their name and they ignore you, you might be inclined, after a few calls, to pick up a stone and toss it at his back. If he still ignores you, you might pick up something heavier to hit him with. That's how God chased me and how I wasn't paying any attention. That was my nightmares and also my actual broken leg. It took a broken leg to get me on the right path.

"I believe fully in demons. I believe they can be God's tools, also. Snakes were one of my demons but through dream study they became friends. Then they became few.

"Evil beings once beat up on me on a regular basis until I asked God to take them away. He did," Vi shivered. "They were very real in my dreams. Who knows where they came from, but God has all power. These words came to me in a dream, 'If you have fear, you have not God.' I looked it up in the Bible. Isaiah 41:10 says, 'So, do not fear, for I am with you.' Remembering this verse served the purpose of bringing this home to me just when I needed it. It made a lot of my worries seem ridiculous."

"Are there things I do that bring the snakes and monsters into my dreams?" I asked.

"There are some things that I've done, innocently enough," Vi replied. "They got me in a lot of trouble. I see devils as many little things that walk into your life when you over indulge. Some are obvious things like alcohol and drugs. Just as fruitful are self-pity, anger, gossip, wrong decisions, and JUDGING. I feel I opened many doors for evil to walk in. I came to believe that God uses them directly to teach us things but they also come indirectly as part of a cause and effect system that God has in place.

"I picture this cause and effect thing like stepping on the tongs of a garden rake that's lying hidden in the grass. It comes up and whacks me in the face. When I wandered aimlessly through life, before dream study, this often happened."

"Vi, that's funny, I haven't seen a garden rake like that in years. I think they were used to hoe the dirt from around the plants, give the roots relief from the weeds and let them breathe. Maybe there's an analogy there, too."

"You're beginning to sound like me," Vi said, "Everything's an analogy but that's dream work. It's good to get your mind working along those lines."

"Do we live more than one life?" That was another one of many things I'd come to think might be true.

Vi answered, "I'll tell you how I came to be a believer in reincarnation. In one dream, I walked through a deserted city of concrete rooftops and tall building tops. I stopped to gaze over a bridge. Four tall buildings, windows below windows, created a chasm below. It reminded me of an empty elevator shaft. I knew life was going on behind those windows and became curious.

"I lifted off the bridge and floated down between the buildings. I passed floor number 10, 9, 8, 7, 6. Suddenly I was at −1, -2. I decided to enter a window at −3. I was on a cobblestone street with narrow sidewalks and three story houses close by. It was much like I'd once seen in Holland. A door opened and wind whisked me inside.

"Inside a woman rushed around, getting a dinner ready. She hollered at me like I was a bad child. There was a father and a brother in the scene. They were fine. Finally I had enough, left by the front door and let the wind whisk me back out the window. I was vaguely aware that in that same instant a horse came galloping down the street and my brother yelled, 'Watch out!'"

"Back in the shaft of windows, I floated up –2, -1, 0, +1, +2 and floated in that window. There I sat in a field of flowers cradling my own angry child in my lap. I loved the child but she required a lot of patience and I knew it was my mother from the other life. Since that dream, I've been a believer in reincarnation."

"So, do you believe natural healing or miracles like laying on of hands work for everyone?" I wanted to know.

"I think it's available," Vi replied, "Miracles do happen but this is one more place where I part with the Metaphysicians. They teach God is abundance (as He is) and they feel saying affirmations will bring this abundance or healing to them. I found that writing those lists in the back of my dream journal serve just as well. My experience is that I needed to earn the good I got. There are a lot of things we can cure. I'll tackle anyone's headache, be it a migraine or not. I find massage very helpful, just getting rid of some stress. When I run my hand over a person's skin I can feel a hot energy coming from a sore spot. It used to amaze my husband when giving him a massage; I could pinpoint the spot where the hurt originated. We don't always know that ourselves until someone touches it.

"Our body is complex and it is teaching us all the time both about our physical states and our emotional and spiritual ailments. It pays to learn to pay attention to your body and act on any warning signs you get. These warnings also will come in dreams. We can avoid a lot of ailments.

"As far as understanding what your dreams are saying, Jung has put us on the right track by showing us how to recognize the power inside dream work, the archetypes, the shadows we've repressed, and the instincts we never stopped to consider. I was able to work with the dreams long before reading Jung. It's all just so much clearer to me now and easier to explain.

"Miracles did happen for me and, no doubt, for others. They happen with more frequency when you meet this mighty power within you half way. God is walking around that prayer table."

I asked, "If God is so all-knowing, why do we even have to interpret dreams. Can't God make clear what He wants us to do?"

"People often ask me that," Vi replied, "I happened on the answer in the Bible: 2 Samuel 12:1-4. The prophet Nathan is sent to tell David a story of a terrible deed. It could have been a nightmare for

David. If so, David woke incensed and wanting to kill the terrible man in the dream (story). Then David was told it was himself who did the terrible deed.

"I wondered why was this fictitious story told to David in the first place? Why wasn't he just told his actions were wrong? Then it came to me. David needed to feel anger because of the deed. He needed to feel to his very core the injustice of it all. He had to know he'd never even entertain doing such a thing.

"I've been through similar things in my dreams. At first the dream didn't seem to be about me, but when I searched for a story within the dream scene, I found a personal change in my attitude. I became surer of my attitude and less wishy-washy. I needed that sureness about myself on many levels.

"We live by feelings much more than intellect. Once I learned to listen, directions are now given to me in a way a lot easier to understand. This was part of the road to health, wholeness and happiness. The road is one Carl G. Jung called individuation."

There was yet another topic on my list. "You mentioned getting messages from the dead," I prompted.

"Sure," Vi replied, "My mother came in a dream and that day I found my sister who I'd not seen in twenty-five years. My brother came back giving me exactly one weeks warning of his wife's new marriage announcement. He and I shared, after he died, instructions that led me to the right time and way to help his eighteen year old son, David, strung out since the age of fourteen on drugs. He came to live with me, cleaned himself up and is today the father of three beautiful little girls and, after working his way up from stock boy, he became an executive with Toys R' Us.

"Do other peoples relatives bring you messages?" I asked.

"Yes," Vi laughed again. "A hairdresser I once met, Tony, lost his father unexpectedly. Tony had things he wished he could tell his father. I offered to dream for him. I learned Tony is a twin. I learned his father died just before Christmas the year before. I learned Tony is gay and I learned that his father made them promise on his deathbed not to sell the family property to Publix Food Stores. Tony knew from all this information I gathered that his father knew all about him, was still watching over him and did not fault him – unless he decided to sell the property to Publix."

"That's fascinating," I said, "Got any other stories?"

Vi went on. "George, from Tennessee, learned from my dreams that his recurring dreams of a father he hated were an apology from his father. We met in an online chat room. He liked something I said and gave me his phone number and asked me to call him collect. I did and ended up dreaming for him and found his father's profession, his father's illness that caused his death and the many hours of sleep his father lost that caused him to make bad decisions like abandoning George at aged nine on the side of the road. The knowledge relieved years of hate and anger for George. He, too, wanted to join his father, in his dreams, fishing – just as they should have done when he was alive."

"Wow! I've heard some sermons you've given in church that you said you got from dreams. You did a couple as plays," I asked, "Have you had dream messages for all of us lately?"

"I had one that said life is a puzzle," Vi replied.

"Don't I know that?" I said.

"Life is a puzzle and we are each a piece of that puzzle," she went on, "I was given the task of assembling a large puzzle, many pieces. Oddly, it was the current front page of that day's newspaper. Two men needed it right away for some presentation. I took up the challenge and just as I was putting the final pieces in place, a child came with a simpler puzzle, all assembled and the men took that one instead,"

"Oh, no. That's probably true though," I said, "People want things easy."

Vi said, "The next dream that same night showed my puzzle laid out on a stretch of dessert. A ground hog approached from the top-left corner of the puzzle and burrowed underneath the entire puzzle. It made its exit back on the ground after the lower right-hand corner and continued on his way across the desert. You could see his path underground as the puzzle pieces moved.

"I believe the first puzzle, being the front page of a current newspaper, was telling me about life today. It's like I've been trying to get a grip on the meaning of life and something's telling me, don't bother. Life is constantly changing. Even if we were so wise as to see the whole picture, others would prefer a simpler version. On one hand it's that thing again that I share with Jung, trying to put things in words people will accept.

"The ground hog going underneath changed the puzzle also. That I take as a hint about the unconscious forces changing the picture also, not just us people.

"The ground hog, representing some people, wants no part of the big picture. He prefers his hot dry journey of life across nothing. He had his head in the sand. I took this to be the people who turned their backs on dream work, meditation, introspection, turned their backs on trying to follow God's plan for whatever reason. The more people we can get to work on being who they were meant to be, the more perfect will be this puzzle of God's. That I call a sermon worth repeating, a worthy message or advertisement for dream work."

"I can see it now," I said, "a puzzle on a billboard, for all to see, saying life's answers are in your dreams."

"You got it," Vi said. "Until we learn to solve our problems and become proper pieces of the puzzle, we are going to keep getting beat up by the hard knocks life hands us."

I laughed. "I think my edges are a little dented."

"There's no end to the messages of this dream," Vi continued. "Another way to look at the puzzle is that Jung was like the 'I' of the dream, trying to assemble life's mysteries. He knew people would prefer a simpler puzzle, all put together for them. His dilemma was, say what he really thought and have his truths set aside, be ridiculed, loose his position in society; or put them in the simpler pattern of psychologists' scientific terms. He could talk of what his heart knew based on his own spiritual experience or hand the world a difficult yet simpler puzzle of archetypes, complexes and animas, hoping someone else would take his beginning and go with it.

"Are you ready to do something with this dream?" I asked.

Vi said, "Sometimes I wonder if I should even bother to put the puzzle together. I fear my thoughts, my truths being set aside for a simpler work. But I can't stop. I think there are a few more people willing to listen."

"How do you go forward?" I wanted to know.

"I take little steps forward," Vi said, "like the course I took certifying me as a leader of dream groups. I know God opens doors when I can best help His plan and this dream course is opening a door to further a passion I've had for a long time. Where it will lead me is up to God. I do know that any change in this world begins in little ways, with each of us.

"I count each of my dreams for other people as a small step forward."

"Vi, first help me understand better how you work with your dreams. Then, I'd love to hear more of those dreams you've had for other people," I said.

Chapter 11

Developing Dream Recall

"Vi, how can I develop my dreams to find help in them? What do you tell people who say or think, they don't dream?" I asked,

"There are several reasons we don't catch our dreams," Vi answered. "One is that our ego thinks he knows everything and refuses to listen to our inner promptings. Ego is the part of us who makes everyday decisions, goes to work, and plays with the kids. Ego, we <u>think</u>, runs our lives.

"Ego is who we think we are, except when something bubbles up unannounced and we wonder, 'Why did I do or say that?' The source could be our true self, according to Jung, or the higher power in us bubbling up from our unconscious trying to get us on a better track. That unknown deep inside us, what Carl Jung called the unconscious, is as much in charge of us as is our ego and, truth be known, maybe more in charge."

"Ego does not hold all knowledge," Vi continued, "Ego often thinks it's doing perfectly fine without delving into the unconscious regions. Those interested in self-study have a humbleness, a yearning for something better, a feeling there's more to this life than we know,"

"I know that feeling," I said

Vi said, "It's a continuing process for me and it's been a bumpy one. Often the things in the unconscious, like who we were meant to be or the things we've repressed, bubble up and cause chaos in our life. One of life's big lessons is to be humble so we can listen and learn. I once worked with a man suffering with terminal cancer who was very much the ego led personality. I'd known him a long time. The cancer taught him humility. Having learned this, I'm sure he's gone on to a better spot in heaven for it."

"I have to know," I asked, "Is this true of all cancer patients?"

"No," Vi said, "As much as we are alike, we are different, but we do all have dreams. Capturing your dreams is not hard. It takes time, patience, and persistence. Have you ever watched a newborn baby's face as it sleeps? It sucks, it twists its mouth, squints it's eyes, kicks. We are born with that ability to dream,"

"My dog dreams," I said.

"Sure, all animals do," Vi replied, "Little people, however, become frightened of dreams. That usually happens between the ages of two and five. With no one around to explain them to us, we make the decision not to dream anymore. The dream function goes deeper and we cease to remember them."

"I can remember trying to help my children with their nightmares," I said, "All I could do was wake them and comfort them."

"That's true for most parents," Vi agreed, "It's too bad we, as parents, aren't better equipped, have more understanding of why these nightmares are happening. Later in life, when we want to bring this ability back, it helps to understand those childhood dreams,"

"Please, tell me about childhood dreams!" I said.

Vi answered, "Growing up we go through a lot more changes, physically and emotionally then we do as adults. Change in a dream is often shown as a death. First beings chase us (they're the new things that want to be in our lives. They want to take us over), then, in the dreams, we die.

"This is a simplified version," Vi said, "Other things cause nightmares like discord in the family, an actual prediction, or past lives, but for most deaths seen in dreams it's like the child who can't tie his/her shoes needs to die before the child who can tie his/her shoes can live. The child who has to have his milk poured for him must die to give life to the child who can pour his\her own milk."

I could understand that. "So death is a good thing!"

"In a dream," Vi said, "If the child recognizes this is a coming, growing change, he/she might be able to speed up the growth process. Say to the child that it means something you can't do now, pretty soon you will be doing it."

Vi continued, "As adults we have fewer things to learn, but it often takes longer to learn the lesson. This gives rise to recurring dreams."

"I've got a couple of them," I said, "I wish you'd take a look at them," This could be neat.

"Sure," Vi agreed, "Most adults I talk to who remember their dreams start the conversation with recurring dreams. If you collect two or more, you can see your own growth even if you perceive no outwardly change."

"I'm getting you off course," I remembered, "Is there more to bringing back the ability to recall dreams?"

"Yes," Vi said, "Bringing back the ability to recover dreams happens slowly like building a muscle. You make a commitment to yourself, you immerse yourself in thinking about dreams, read and talk about dreams. During the day I used to say to myself, 'This could be a dream'. I remember joking with my husband as we shook out sheets, both of us saying this could be a dream. It worked. I actually saw my hands in a dream that night and knew I was dreaming. It was exciting without even waking up."

I remembered something another dream worker had told me. "Isn't that what is called Lucid Dreaming?" I asked.

"Yes," Vi said, "That's what they call it and that's another subject. Anyway, I keep a pad and pencil next to my bed. In the beginning, before going to bed I'd drink a large glass of water and repeat to myself, 'I will remember my dreams, I will remember my dreams'.

"As I awakened to the call of nature," Vi continued, "I stayed still. In my mind, I'd replay what was just going through it. I did it a couple of times. Then I could take pad and pen to the bathroom with me and write it in there. If I move so much as a hand or turn my head before this replay, the dream will flit away forever."

"Boy," I said, "I know that feeling!"

Vi continued, "In the beginning, I'd get only one word or just a feeling or something may have gone through my mind I didn't think was worthy of remembering, but I wrote it down anyway. I was building that muscle.

"Sometimes the dumbest dream stories hold a big message, too! One dream had me sitting in a chair with a long old-fashioned skirt. I watched while mice played around my feet. I decided it wouldn't hurt to scale back my expectations in life. I was beginning to feel real good at the time. 'Poor as a church mouse,' was the reminder that the mice gave me. I decided to be happy with just having my needs fulfilled, no grandiose schemes. Actually, I could never in a hundred years have perceived I'd ever be teaching others about dreams."

I wondered, "Do new people to your dream group need to be catching their dreams?"

"No," Vi said, "When my dream group first started meeting, they'd come with no dreams to interpret. They'd use my dreams or we'd take some from a book. It wasn't long before everyone would come with a dream. Now they often have to save some for the next week."

"I'm thinking of all the times I've wakened, knowing I had a dream, but can't recall it," I said.

Vi said, "You can still benefit if you don't remember a dream. Pay attention to your mood when you wake up. If you are exhausted or unhappy, you may have been warring with your higher self over some action you took the day before or you plan to take. When you wake happy, perhaps your higher self is content with the way you're living your life. You still can find clues to working with Spirit."

I'd been looking at a strange assortment of items that seemed to have a prominent position on top of a bookcase in her home. "I see you have a rather odd collection of statues, Vi. You have it set up like a shrine to something," I said.

Vi laughed, "That's one of the ways I honor the dreams I remember, my dream image collection. I'd ignored the dreams for a long time and felt a need to confirm my commitment. In the beginning it was like saying to God, 'I'm hearing you, I'm trying,'"

"How neat. You have statues, drawings, poems, crosses, angels, candles," I named some of them.

Vi agreed, "Jeremy Taylor, author of 'Where People Fly and Water Runs Uphill,' writes his dreams in an artist's sketchbook. He writes them in various colors. He adds a paragraph or two in black about things in life that either parallel his dreams or hold high energy for him. He glues in newspaper clippings, makes drawings illustrating the dreams or clips objects from other sources. The cover is covered with clippings illustrating dream images. What a living history these books are. Someday I'll start a book like that."

I picked up a drawing. "So this was a dream you had?"

Vi nodded yes, "You'd be surprised at the new understanding it opens. When you see it in a picture rather than words on a page, a line of cars turns into a backbone. A row of lighted windows become musical notes on a staff. The food cans are representative of things I've either added or eliminated from my diet because of a dream."

"I wondered about them," I laughed, "You don't often see food cans on display."

"That's why they're kind of hidden in the back," Vi laughed with me, "I really don't need that reminder anymore. Probably time to get rid of them. Another opportunity to honor the dream I think is interesting is when some one I know is in my dream, I call or write that person and tell them about it. I present it as an amusing story. Then I leave it with them. I did that to a man who owned the grocery store in this little town I used to live in. In a dream, I was attending a birthday party for him. (I didn't know him that well.) His father came and told me his son was going to run for president. He could have anything he wanted. I wrote it in a letter to him. He wrote back thanking me for the dream and later told me it gave him the strength to open his second store. He felt he was getting the go-ahead from his dead father. From then on, I try always to contact the person,"

"I wake up with songs going through my mind," I said.

Vi smiled, "If a song goes through your mind, first think on the words of the song. Do they pertain to something in your life? If not, spend more time singing, playing an instrument, or just listening to music,"

"Sometimes they're so coincidently funny," I laughed, "I had promised to help a neighbor with a garage sale and woke up that morning singing, 'If I were a rich man. Ta-da-da-da-da-da-da-da-da-da-deddle-dum'."

"That is funny," Vi agreed, "It may be a wish, but singing can show contentment. Maybe you're content. Sometimes that's more important than money."

I said, "Yes, I'm content. Not rich. What about the real long dreams? These are a story in themselves, complete from beginning to end."

Vi suggested, "Write your experience into a poem, a song. An essay, a play."

I went on, "These are dreams that are like movie epics. They come complete with beginning, middle and end, all in the same night. What would you do with them?"

Vi said, "These usually become the sermons. Usually they hold a universal message that most everyone can benefit from. I write them, not always intending to use them, but if a need should arise, I have them."

"What if I miss a message, knew I dreamed, but for one reason or another didn't retain it?" I asked,

"If I miss a message," Vi said, "it comes again in another dream, a different story, until I do get the message. Sometimes something happens during the day and a light bulb goes off in my mind and I think 'this is what that dream was about'."

"Vi," I was curious, "Some people have some pretty dramatic trauma in their past. Does that come up and how do you handle it? I'm thinking of victims of sex crimes or the things soldiers have witnessed."

"The dreams use what you know to tell you other things, things you need to be aware of in your future," Vi said, "They'll bring up a similar instance from your past. Many of us have something in the past that we feel had best stay buried. First, you have to remember, God will not bring up a past problem in our dreams unless we're ready to face it and solve it. Many a night I woke up repeating, 'He won't give me more than I can handle'. "

We both paused, thinking about possible past problems. Then Vi continued, "I find that time is a great healer. As you put new experiences in your life, your dreams begin to change and if the new experiences are pleasant ones, the nightmares become fewer."

"Vi, you said recurring dreams were one of the first things people ask about, but I bet nightmares run a close second," I guessed.

"The recurrence usually is the nightmare," Vi said.

"Okay," I started to wrap it up, "So I put my paper and pencil next to my bed, drink the water, try to be ready to face any nightmares for the sake of learning something to eventually get rid of the nightmares. I've kicked old ego aside, realized I don't have all the answers, I remember all the good that came from your experience and hope it's there for me. Is there anything else to know?"

Vi answered, "I've often hesitated to tell my story for fear people will go into this expecting a reward. Just keep an open mind. Opportunities came to me. Once you clear your subconscious mind of all the useless stuff it's been carrying, something has to fill that space.

I think expecting some good is all right. Who knows what is waiting inside you for development that will help the whole world.

"You might have it in you to be a great inventor. Where would we be without the inspiration great inventors have credited their dreams? For example, Elias Howe of sewing machine fame was struggling to find a way to get the thread to lock through the material. In his dreams he was in a huge bubbling pot surrounded by hungry savages poking him with spears. In the dream he noticed the spears had holes in their tips. He woke with his answer.

"Paul McCartney, Billy Joel and Beethoven have found inspiration from their dreams. Some hear musical arrangements, while others hear lyrics."

Vi continued, "It's reported that golfer Jack Nicklaus found a new way to hold his golf club in a dream, which he credits as significantly improving his golf game."

"Can you recommend a book," I asked, "to help me find those kind of facts about dreams that I can hold onto?"

"Yes!" Vi said eagerly and picked up a book I'd noticed in the bookshelves. "Try this, *Our Dreaming Mind*, by Robert Van De Castle, Ph.D.

"It was published in 1994 and sets down just about everything anyone would want to know about the history of dreams regarding the various cultures, religions, past research, present research and the practical use of dreams in science, music, art, and math. I first learned the sewing machine story there and have heard it repeated several places since. Let me read a bit to you."

Vi read, "The most famous account of creative scientific dreaming is associated with Fredrich A. von Kekule, a professor of chemistry at Ghent, Belgium. Kekule had been attempting for some time to solve the structural riddle of the benzene molecule. He fell asleep in a chair and began to dream of atoms flitting before his eyes, forming various structures and patterns. Eventually some long rows of atoms formed and began to twist in a snakelike fashion. Suddenly, one of the snakes seized hold of its tail and began to whirl in a circle. Kekule awoke 'as if by a flash of lightening' and began to work out the implications of his dream imagery. He constructed a model of a closed ring with an atom of carbon and hydrogen at each point of a hexagon. This discovery revolutionized organic chemistry. It is not surprising that when Kekule was describing his dream-discovered insight to a scientific convention in 1890, he concluded his presentation by urging the audience, 'Let us learn to dream, gentlemen, and then we may perhaps find the truth.'"

"Wow!" I said.

"Listen to this paragraph," Vi continued, "One Nobel Prize winner in physiology and medicine, Albert von Szent-Gyorgyi, acknowledged in regard to research problems, 'My brain must continue to think about them when I sleep because I wake up, sometimes in the middle of the night, with answers to questions that have been puzzling me.'"

"Is there anything on religion and various cultures and dreams?" I asked.

"All of that," Vi replied, "Listen to this. Aside from their role in the development of specific religions, dreams have suggested answers to many pervasive and eternal questions. Who are we? Where did we come from? Why are we here? Of what are we made? Where are we going? What is death? Is there existence after death? If there is existence, of what does it consist? People of all times have pondered these tenacious and troubling questions. What is seldom recognized is that dreams have helped to provide some answers."

"I can't wait to get to sleep tonight," I said.

"You'll have a dream," Vi assured me, "Have your pad and pencil ready. Don't move when you wake up. Just keep going over the scene as you slowly wake up. Play it again and again. After the third time, turn over and write it. It gets easier. I sometimes get up in the morning and write five or six dreams. Build that muscle, build your life. Each person who does this adds to the good energy of the world."

"I believe you," I said, "I'd sure like to hear more about those dreams you've had for other people."

"I've got a few of them," Vi said, "Settle in and I'll not only share some of the stories, but I'll tell you some of the things I've learned about dreams by doing that."

I was shocked, "You say there's more to learn? You must mean some tips on interpreting."

"More," Vi laughed, "There's more about interpreting, more about peoples' essence, and more about understanding the flow of the stories from midnight to rising. You might be surprised at the things I learn about people, the messages they need to know, what things we might think are important that are not number one on God's list."

Part Two
Dreams For Others

Part 2

I WILL DREAM FOR YOU

"In these dreams I had for other people,
Take a look at their questions for God,
The answers God gives that you might benefit from,
The facts of their lives I had no way of knowing that proves my mind was in their realm,
The peaks into their essence,
How God might have a different view of what's important for them right now.

Time after time,
The advice is not something I would give --
But it rings truer than anything I could say.

The advice comes with a force that changes the minds of the person involved

Much more than my words could trigger."

This section written by Vi.

Chapter 12

Feed My Babies

After reading some of my writings on line, someone named Cindy e-mailed me a message that sounded urgent, frantic, and desperate.

"Please give me something I can use to keep my head above water, to keep a roof over my children's heads. I am going nowhere fast and am so close to the edge it is terrifying. I've exhausted all avenues to no avail and feel like I'm falling in a downward spiral. I don't do drugs and I have faith. I try to be a positive influence on all around me, but I can't do even the simple things like buying school supplies for my children or keeping food on our table. I'm sorry for dumping on you but I'm desperate. I'm not asking for a handout. I need something to hold on to, to build on for some kind of a future. I'm so sick of the negative, greedy people I see every day. Please help me."

That night, I held her request in my hand and prayed for God to give me the practical advice she needed.

The first dream shows pictures on the walls that are hung crookedly. My (her) job is to straighten them up. I do it with my thoughts. I think one straight and they all move. It frightens me and I wake up.

In sharing this vision with her I related that I saw a lack of persistence. She could have stayed and straightened the pictures with her power. She agreed persistence was a big problem for her. She had many excuses, no time, no money, and no education in the right places. She often felt if she'd just persisted in this or that, she'd have a better life today. The fear I felt when the pictures moved showed the power she has but is afraid to put to use.

The second dream is in a cottage (her small life). I see a lot of sheet music spread across the floor. A young girl comes to help pick up. She begins singing the songs. I harmonize with her. The dream goes on to other things, suggestions for her future but the big thing is right here.

I had no way of knowing that she is a singer. She sings in nursing homes. The fact that someone was helping her clean up was a measure of hope from her mess.

Then I see her involved with the spirit of trees, grass, plants and such. They sing together as they clean up a natural area (bushes, plants, walks). He says that as long as she works with Him, he will harmonize with her.

Volunteer time! She was already doing this and perhaps coming in touch with me was a reward. Now she knows He is helping her. She answered back, about this dream, that she'd had an affinity for nature since childhood. She spent many hours sitting in a tree and talking to the tree. Something else I did not know about her.

This last dream shows her lack of faith. To me it is her lack of listening to God and believing what she was hearing. It is an edict to build on her music and concentrate more on life's positive things.

However desperate life may sometimes seem, it is part of our journey. Part of the game of life is to learn to enjoy the journey. She is gathering experience for her calling.

Since part of the dreams had mentioned volunteering, I suggested she do as much of that as she could because then she'd be opening doors for God's plan to manifest. It is sometimes good to be dissatisfied with life because you keep growing as you reach for that nitch only you can fill. I suggested she adopt an attitude of gratitude for whatever positive she saw each day. Say thanks out loud. Her children are learning from her, to say thanks, to be grateful, to find joy in small things. I also suggested she make want lists with her children and cross off items as she either received them or changed her wants. This would also make it easier for them to know Mom could not always get what they wanted immediately.

She and I both knew someone greater than us had touched us. Someone or thing told me things about her life I would have no way of knowing. She now knew a Spirit from God was helping her, giving her strength, guiding her footsteps. We each need to get to know the Spirit that surrounds us, have a better grasp of what is good for us and what is not.

Chapter 13

Adult Daughters!

Nichole asked about her relationship with her twenty-nine year old daughter and her three-year-old granddaughter. We'd discussed all the ifs, ands and buts of the situation over lunch. Still, she asked me to dream for her and I went home wondering what else could be said?

In our material world, people can give all the advice they want but taking it and following it are completely different matters. Something has to click in your heart to make you want the change in yourself. It starts in your soul. That's why you can't change anyone else!

That night I found that Spirit still had something else to say. It may have been Spirit. It may have been her daughter's and granddaughter's guardian angels, spirit guides, and\or higher consciousness. I present the story as it happened. You can draw your own conclusions. It happened, and it made a positive change in Nichole's life.

The truth of the dreams made a difference. She went from being a stressed out mother and grandmother to being a lady with peace and love in her heart and room to move on with her own life. I'm sure this made her much easier to love. The truth involved past lives, choosing one's parents before birth and a communication with a much smarter being.

I interpret dreams and visions for other people to the best of my ability but it's their life. They recognize the truth faster than I, because they've lived it. Things I say might jog a memory, clear up a dream story.

This time, as I lay my head on my pillow, I learned I did not have to be asleep to get messages. I simply needed to move my own thoughts aside and sort of put them on a shelf somewhere because a letter quickly started to be dictated to me from Nichole's daughter's higher power.

"Dear Mom,

I am where I am, due to choices I've made. I need to learn my own lessons. You brought me up with a strong strength of will. My daughter gives me a purpose. I weigh the strengths and weaknesses of the people I meet. The good I see sinks in to blend with what I know and will come to fruition when I am ready. I must do this on my own."

I asked, "Why did Deana choose Nichole to be her mother?"

"I knew Nichole would have a spiritual outlook and would be able – because she loved me - to give me the space to learn lessons connected with Chris. Chris and I were together in a past life. I let him down then. I need to make it up to him this time.
Love, Deana"

Dream #1: Nichole and I are going from family to family to see what it takes to make their lions roar. Don't let the lion roar. Dad will be angry.

Dream #2: Nichole and I are now visiting an Indian brothel for the experience of writing about it. We talk our way out of going through indecent acts. The men are comical. All the people are nice, just doing what they are meant to do. The men are all dressed in long underwear (my term "long johns"). They have a flap in the back to go to the bathroom, buttons all the way up the front, legs and sleeves to the ankles and wrists. We work our way down a hall visiting every room and then go back to the beginning.

At 4 AM: I asked about Nichole's future. My physical feeling was of dryness. I got out of bed and got a drink of water but that did not quench my thirst. The dry cough made my throat seem scratchy. I worried about catching a cold but then realized it was a dream vision about Nichole's future – she shouldn't worry herself into ill health!

As I went back to sleep, another letter to Nichole came through my mind.
Dear Mom,

There is a love between us that transcends many lifetimes, and many in-between lifetimes. When you can stop feeling responsible for my life, I can long for the happy times we used to have, we will be a very close mother \ daughter team once again. This day will come for us both.

Dream #3: At a street fair, Nichole walks up behind a table of goods. A manikin is standing there, dressed as a man from the twenties. He wears a black suit, white shirt with a tight neck, black round hat. She stands beside him as if to be another manikin. He acknowledges her and walks away. I heard an owl hoot once.

My thoughts were that this man was a spirit with whom she would be able to communicate. Things were not as they seemed. If he was her male side, the one who made decisions rather than ponder on them some more, he was ready to move on. The street fair may be pointing out the variety of things available when you see them. Life is not just one table.

Then another letter started to be dictated through me.
"Dear Grandmother,

I chose Mom to be my mother this time. I love you but you could not help me learn the things, have the experiences, that Mom can. Please understand. Thank you for being a part of my world because I know you're there, that is enough.

Encourage my potential. Never let me forget the good I can achieve. Grandmothers are good for that. Love, Me."

After having the dreams and discussing them, Nichole decided to back off when she was inclined to give advice to her daughter. She relaxed, knowing that Deana would be fine. She would be there if and when her daughter asked for help. They began family outings on a friendlier basis. Nichole listened and praised.

The dream about the Indian brothel reflected Nichole's far distant heritage. Perhaps it was time for her to investigate this corner of herself, learn more about the American Indian beliefs. She said it was also the validation I said would come through. In her possessions were two sets of Long Johns that once belonged to her grandfather. There was my confirmation. Also, the name Chris was true. I didn't know that.

Nichole had heard from her daughter and her granddaughter in words they never could say themselves. These dreams raise some interesting points. It seems these children lived before, they chose their parents and their higher consciousness knows the truth of what their life is about. We all, through our dreams, have access to this information of our higher conscious. It is the way God created our complicated world. Part of our spiritual growth is realizing these truths, and using them to draw closer to our Creator.

The angels were proud she had
begun the search that would
draw her closer to what God
wanted for her.

Chapter 14

Will We Ever Marry?

Gary and Ali approached me for a dream at a church I had been attending for a couple of years. So they weren't complete strangers to me. They were engaged, then not engaged, engaged, not engaged. They both appeared in their early thirties and were the darlings of the congregation long before I began coming there. They both were always well dressed. He was always in suits and she in nice dresses and heels. They appeared to be prosperous.

I was one of few white people in this predominately black church. Gary and Ali took me under their wings from the first, sat with me and made me feel at home. Whatever their relationship problem was, they didn't share that with me until they asked for this dream. Their question was: Would they ever marry each other?

They each wanted separate dreams so Ali went first. I held the paper with her name and address in my hand before sleeping and prayed to God to shine some light on this situation.

As I fell asleep, in that state of half sleep, half awake, a song began going through my mind. "Don't go chasing waterfalls. Stick to the rivers and lakes that you're used to."

Writing this on my pad I wondered, was she expecting some excitement in life that she wasn't getting in this relationship? Should the meandering river, the placid lake be the situation she was in now? She would know. I went back to sleep.

The first dream usually restates the question. I think this first dream gave Ali a lot of food for thought. It opened some doors for her to understand her motivations, because they did eventually get married.

The first dream found me sitting in a couple's living room. He is playing piano. I am amazed at his talent. I praise him when he stops and then a woman walks in. She announces that the marriage is over. I am shocked!

95

In waking life, this is where the situation was. I was shocked as they seemed perfect for each other. In the dream, since it was for Ali, all figures and things are her. So if the 'I' was shocked, she was shocked also. The truth of the dream, the verification that I was in her realm was the little known fact that Gary had an interest in music.

The dream continued. Another couple comes into the room. Their marriage is over, too. He'd instructed her take their boat on a trailer and to put it away for the winter. It was a lot of work and responsibility. She didn't like that.

Yes, Ali did not like the thought of added future responsibility.

The dream went on. Another couple take us through a store they are abandoning. We can have anything we want. It is full of statuary, decorating knick-knacks. The others choose easily. I feel strange. These things represent a thriving business. I'd seen a black wrought-iron piece that had realistic ivy wrapped around it. When pressed I say I'll take that. We search and search for it but now can't find it. That was the end of that dream.

If the business is their marriage, why abandon it when it is thriving? The statuary and knick-knacks, to me, were remnants of a long past they were willing to abandon. Memories. Giving away may also be a peek at their generous natures.

After writing this much, I lay my head back and a vision came. It was a quick look at a work island in a kitchen. It is clean with beautiful shiny Formica, ready to be used. Drawing back I see a floor of scattered debris. We are walking away from it. It would have been a wonderful place to work.

My waking feeling, as I wrote the vision was, "No! Don't walk away!"

Next came another song, "Matilda, Matilda, She takes me money and runs Venezuela." Hmmmmm.

The last dream has me going up stairs. A woman follows me demanding, "Marry him! You better marry him!"

Then came another song. "The quiet walks, the noisy fun, the ballroom prize we almost won. We'll have these moments to remember. The laughter we were glad to share, we'll have these moments to remember."

Lastly, these words came, "Make the right decision, the rest will fall into place."

It was 5:45 A.M... I was frustrated, "Gee whiz, God," I said. "This was my original question. What is the right decision?"   I was evidently through for the night as there were no more dreams or visions. Maybe Gary's dream the next night would give me a better answer.

The next night I took Gary's paper with his information and essence to bed with me. It was the same question for God. Would they ever marry each other?   The difference between the two nights of dreams would seem stereotypical of women and men. Ali's was all about family, commitment, responsibility. Gary took me to the circus.

In dream one I (and I took the 'I' figure to be Gary) am to be left alone to do what I want to do. I wave goodbye as Ali drives away. My attention turns to the activity taking place in my own backyard. It is a huge, dry, dusty, dirty area. People are training horses for circus performances.

First I read the notices on the wall, then walk through a door to better observe the horses going through their various routines. Some are attached to wagons, some are being led by costumed girls, some are being ridden. My presence bothers them. The horses become out of control when they see me.   Time after time I run for a wall or fence to climb before they can crash into me. The handlers always fight to control the horses. I don't get hurt but I think the animal handlers are very inept at their jobs. I escape to another area of training, drawn there by my curiosity.

Suddenly, I see a group of several large horses harnessed together. They charge into a factory door. I pray for the workers inside. Finally the horses charge back out.

I wondered, could Gary have a variety of control problems? The beauty of dreams is that this is between Gary and his unconscious. I didn't need to know. He would know.

The scene shifts and now I'm inside. I see several curtained off dressing rooms.   Oh how embarrassed I'd be if caught there by someone undressing! I dash through to the next area.

Gary did get embarrassed about my suggestion of loss of control. He went out of his way, as did Ali, to assure me this was not an issue in their relationship.

Next I am watching elephants being trained to walk around partitions. One has seen me and makes a move to stampede me. I dash out again. Every animal wants to hurt me, gets wild in my presence.

I wondered if Gary needed training, if he balked at authority.

I then peek in a small auditorium. Children are being trained to be a good audience. I realize that this training is what I really need. Than I can train others to be good audiences.

When reading this Gary shared that he had been offered an opportunity at work to train new employees. He turned it down but would see if the position was still open.

Dream number two is perhaps a vision of one possible future. I noticed it wasn't anything about the question he'd originally asked. I've gotten this kind of answer before. It's like God is telling us to put things in their right order.

In the next dream, Gary arrives home alone. He and a lover have broken up. There is one thing left unsaid but he feels he cannot go and say it to her because he has a small dog to take care of. A person comes who can care for the dog and Gary then goes the short distance to his ex-lover's home to give her the message. Passion rekindles and he stays.

My feeling is that the small dog is his career path Gary needs to be on. If he takes the opportunity to train the new employees and leaves things in God's hand, all will be alright.

Dream number three has Gary looking in a mirror. A voice behind him says he has some news about his brother. His three children have been taken away from him. Gary is shocked and saddened beyond belief. Questions flood his mind. Who? What? "I won't name names," the voice says, "But I wanted you to know."

Gary whips around and it is his brother sitting behind him. He does not appear sad at all. (Gary has no brother.)

This last dream is presented to show the shock and hurt he'd feel if he let Ali get away. My belief is that Gary is being told to set priorities.

Gary shared that he has tried many jobs to develop a career. It's been like a circus, often with bad results. When I drew a picture of the whole dream, from the note board, to the horse training, thru the factory, the dressing room, the elephant area, the classrooms, he ended up back at the note board looking for new opportunities advertised there. The drawing was of a circle. He'd come full circle. It was time to settle down. If it were my dream …. Gary and Ali have seen the truth, and as I said earlier, they are, finally, happily married.

" Don't dismiss dreams
because of
embarrassment
or guilt.."

Chapter 15

I Didn't Tell Dad

As so often happens at my first meeting with someone new, Tony and I were soon discussing dreams.

I walked into his place of business to buy furniture. Tony is a 20-year-old single man who lives with his mother. Together, with some other family members, they operate a business they've owned for two generations.

"My father died about a year ago," Tony said, "There's so much I wish I'd said to him. I wonder if he's trying to speak to me. Could you ask?"

"Certainly," I said, Actually, when someone asks, the dreams always come. "I'll write out the dreams and let you interpret them," I told him, "I'd be interested in knowing if anything in the dreams makes sense to you. I'd really appreciate some feedback."

"No problem," Tony said, "I have a lot of dreams, myself. I never knew they had meaning. I'd like to learn more about this."

"The stories can be very direct about something going on in your life or they may be symbolic," I warned, "If you're involved in a war in the dream, you look at your life. See where you're in battle with yourself or others. When nightmares occur you are being shown what will happen if you continue on your current path. You make the connection, you change the outcome."

"That's interesting and makes sense," Tony said, "I'd like to see it work."

"Another thing," I said, "Is to look for a 'play on words.' For instance, if the dream story has a character wearing a mask, look for someone who may be putting up a false front. God can be very clear when you understand this symbolic language. A young lady I know was shown to me in a dream as wearing a false chest plate. We laughed over that one because she always wanted bigger breasts. Her false front was poking fun at her for kidding herself about something or possibly hiding something that was close to her heart.

"Back to dreaming for you," I told Tony, "I need to know what time you will be going to sleep."

"Wow, that may be a problem," Tony replied, "I'm going to a party tonight. I'll try to get home early."

"We'll just take it as it comes," I replied, "If the early dreams are not about you, we'll know you weren't asleep."

I went to bed about 10 P.M., holding Tony's paper in my hands. I first woke around 2 A.M. to a force, or wind.

It was what I call a vision. It felt like a blast of air from someone's mouth. The force was so strong I felt it was more than one person. Whoa, I thought, does Tony have a twin? Perhaps it was his father walking in. If so, he must have been a strong personality and been waiting impatiently to speak to his son.

Immediately I regained my senses and knew that I must record these dreams and thoughts. As I wrote I heard a phrase of a song. "You and you alone bring out the gypsy in me," The song is an old one entitled, "My Sweet Embraceable You." Then I went back to sleep.

In the dream I feel frustrated, unable to handle something. It is a holiday. A guest, a very important lady, comes to spend the night.

Other families around us have wonderful celebrations, but I can't handle getting ready for ours.

Clean clothes, fresh from the wash, are piled everywhere. My husband comes in and drops dirty clothes on top of them. We argue. Our guest takes over. She sets the table with a Christmas cake I'd made. Sleep doesn't seem to matter to her.

My husband tosses the gifts aside. Angry, he lays on the floor, his life draining out of him.

Thieves break in to rob us. We all fight them and finally win.

My thoughts on writing this were that perhaps something worth fighting for is needed to make life worth living. It is just my guess.

In the second dream we are living in a borrowed fire truck. It is against the rules and we try to hide the truck so the fire chief won't get into trouble.

As I watch the faces of the other firemen, I see they are definitely going to cause trouble. The chief discusses building a wooden structure around the fire truck to disguise it. He shows us others who've done the same. They will build it for us.

We come home to what looks like a large "Trojan" cow, white with big brown spots. Our home is next to it, in a box.

Writing, I have no clue as to any meaning. I hope it makes sense to Tony.

In dream #3 we stand in line at a checkout counter in the local branch of a chain of hardware stores. Several people ahead of me can not pronounce the name of the store. The cashier doesn't like them and treats them badly, cheats them.

The man ahead of me asks for a confirmation on the pronunciation. I say it for him, as I had heard it in the store's expensive ads on T.V.

The man is so angry he puts money on the counter and leaves.

I'm in a hurry, too. My purchase is less than $20.00 and I am in a hurry to get out of there. The dream ended.

Writing it down, I'm even more clueless. In the morning I typed the dreams and delivered them to Tony's place of business.

He read the dreams and called me. "The time you felt the strong presence was about the time I was going to bed. I was having a great time at the party. About 1 A.M., I remembered you were going to dream for me. I rushed out of there and home feeling very bad about staying out so late," Tony said.

"That's a new experience for me, being awakened because my subject just went to bed. Thanks," I replied,

"Didn't you know I had a twin?" he asked.

"No, I didn't," I replied, stunned.

"I have no idea about the song, never heard it," Tony said, "Did you have any ideas about that? Can you get me a copy of it?"

"I'll try," I said. One thought was the gypsy part. "Did your family come from Spain not too long ago? Maybe it has something to do with a Gypsy background?"

"Mom and Dad came over from Spain right after they were married," Tony said, "There were no Gypsies in the family as far as I know, though."

"The next dream," Tony continued, "Is very much like our lives. Dad died just before Christmas. It wasn't a good time for us. We've been greatly worried about the business, worried about paying the bills. We don't know if we can handle things without Dad."

He continued, "The part about fighting for our lives and the last dream about the hardware store are definitely from Dad. On his deathbed he made us promise never to sell our property to that same company. They own everything all around us and have been trying to get Dad to sell. He made us promise never to sell our land to them. I think he is reminding us of this in this dream. At least that's what my Mom said when she read it.

Tony continued, "The fire department dream is me. Frankly, my hormones are running away with me, like a fire out of control. I don't want to shock you. The dream spoke of breaking the rules and hiding the fact. That's me. I'm gay.

"Because of my upbringing and my family's position in the community, my life style could be a huge embarrassment for them. We could lose our business. I hope you will keep my confidence."

"You don't need to tell me anything. I've quite enough information to convince anyone I was in your subconscious already," I replied, "When I do talk about the dream, I'll certainly change the name and the location."

"The fire engines in this dream speak of my passion. To be quite blunt, building the Trojan cow speaks of the way I need to protect myself. I wonder if Dad is telling me that, too?"

Tony added, "I have to share this with you because it is all so clear to me it makes me laugh,"

We met again a month later and he asked me to dream again and shared that he'd attempted dreaming for others also. Several times since our first meeting he's come to me for help in interpreting his dreams for others. He definitely can do it.

I do not judge anyone. He has the gift and is using it to help others. As it says in the Bible, God is his judge, not me. The practice of non-judgment was made clear to me by contact with this charming twenty-year-old, intelligent, business-like, very passionate and compassionate young man.

While looking up the spelling for 'embraceable' to write this chapter, I discovered the old French derivative, embrasseor, means to instigate or set on fire. That's Tony's essence. It's also the theme of the fire engine story.

*   *   *

Since we seem to be on the subject of sex in dreams, this might be a good time to add an observation of mine. Men, in particular, and certain age groups, tend to dismiss discussions of dreams because their dreams seem to center on the very private world of sex, hence, are very embarrassing.

There is much more going on in these dreams than sex or unfulfilled desires. As with any analogy, we must look to the action of the dream. Are you reaching for something that is taking too much time and taxing your physical energy? One main purpose of dreams is to warn us of overexerting our bodies, or being on the brink of serious illness.

In the dream, is someone taking unfair advantage of you? It could be a warning of some action in your waking life that could seriously injure you.

Your partner in this dream could represent some aspect of yourself. In a dream we should view all people and all things as part of ourselves. Put yourself in that role. What might that person or thing be trying to tell you? If a co-worker was your partner, how do you view this person? Is he/she creative, ambitious, lucky? This aspect, visible so far only in your subconscious mind, may be about to make a breakthrough into your waking life.

Don't dismiss dreams because of embarrassment or guilt. If you keep a journal, you will find a way to write the dream without denigrating yourself and still remember the action later.

As for Tony's father, dead people do come through. They are not gone forever. John 8:51 quotes Jesus as promising, "Most assuredly, I say to you, if anyone keeps My word he shall never see death,"

"This means a lot to me and I will help you in your work with others. Bye for now."

Chapter 16

I Lost My Son

Life after death, heaven, and spiritual communications make for interesting discussions when a day in the office is moving rather slowly. Joni works in the same office as I. A short time after she started there, we got into just such a discussion. Her interest stemmed from the fact that she had lost her only son in an auto accident several years before. The only reminder she had left of him was a beautiful grandson being raised far away.

Danny, her son, was never far from her mind. The loss, pain and love never leave you. A lot of her thoughts were 'what ifs'. If he had lived, what might life had been like? She asked if I could get validation from him that he was okay. She wanted to know what he was doing. If communication was still possible, as I had been saying it was, she wanted to hear from her son, get some reassurance that he'd moved on, gotten a life, but she wondered if he still remembered her.

I had her write her name, address and phone number on a piece of paper that I would hold as I go to sleep. We were not disappointed.

In the dream, chosen by him, I am playing the part of a TV talk show host and he is the person being interviewed. Joni is the unnamed audience. He is delightful. He makes motions with his hands indicating squares. Not knowing whether to laugh at him or if there is a serious intent for his actions, such as four square sides representing balance, I say, "They are interesting but your mother wants to hear from you," He asks for paper and pencil and draws more squares. Finally he calms down and talks.

"I am with her a lot," he says, "I want her to be as happy as I am. That's why we are doing this TV show. She loves TV and you, Vi, can be our in-between interviewer any time. This means a lot to me and I will help you in your work with others. Bye for now."

That was short and fun. I typed it up and took it to Joni the next day. She was turned into a total believer. A secret message had come through. She immediately recognized the squares as boxes. He had been a collector of boxes as far back as she could remember, and only she would know that.

His use of the two TV anchor chairs, the lights and cameras were great fun and apropos. I believe he was also sending a message to his mother to put more fun in her life.

About a year later, Joni asked for another communication from Danny. True to his promise to help me with other projects, he showed me greeting young people in a new church I have been attending. He must have been watching me. The church people are looking for a new place to meet and he shows me a place in the dream.

Knowing we would need validation that he was visiting me and this was not all just a rerun of my current life, he rides through the scene on a motor scooter. He is having a lot of fun. He stops for conversation and talks about a cruise Joni and I had been planning together and her yen to take a trip to England. He says these kinds of things are important. He asks what I'd like to do. I mention a barbershop chorus performance I have tickets to and a certain movie I'd like to see. He said, "Go. Do it!"

I typed it out and took it to Joni even though it might be said this was all a hashing over of her and my current lives. Joni laughed immediately. She saw the secret message that validated her son. The motor scooter was something he'd desperately wanted. He actually got one once only to have a neighbor take it away because Danny was making a nuisance of himself with it. It sat in that man's garage forever, never returning to Danny. In heaven, he now had the privilege of riding one as much as he liked.

I woke with a song going through my mind – also from Danny. "Look for the silver lining, when ere a cloud appears in the sky. Remember somewhere, the sun is shining, and so the right thing to do is make it shine for you. A heart full of joy and gladness will always banish sadness and strife. So always look for the silver lining and try to find the sunny side of life."

Real closure was brought when he appeared in one of Joni's own dreams. She asked, "What does it mean when he turns his back on me and walks through a door? He closed it behind him."

"He's coming back into this world," was my reply.

Chapter 17

He Died.
How Can I Keep On Living?

A few nights after a speech before a Parents Without Partners meeting I sat with a stack of requests for dream readings. My fingers kept returning to Mary's business card. I picked up the phone and called her.

"Mary, sorry to call you so late. You gave me a note after my speech last week. Would you still like to talk about your dreams?"

"Yes, most definitely," Mary excused herself. I could hear her blow her nose. I hoped I'd not picked a bad time. "Vi, thank you for calling. Your timing couldn't be better. I believe strongly in dream messages because some of my own dreams have come true,"

Mary's words tumbled out, "Lately my dreams have featured waterfalls and rivers. I understand these are very spiritual. Perhaps they contain an important message, but I don't understand what I'm getting."

"My husband died of cancer about a year ago," she continued. "It's not like we didn't have time to prepare for it. We knew for years. I've been praying God would tell me what my purpose is on this earth. Surely it wasn't to suffer like this. If He's trying to talk to me through my dreams, I'm not remembering enough of them to understand."

"I'll be glad to dream for you," I said when she took a breath. "I'll call you in the morning and hopefully we'll know what it is you are supposed to be doing with your life."

Next morning we shared the dreams by phone. Then I typed them and mailed them to her. We'd know even more about the truths found in the dreams when Mary could actually read the words. This was my letter to her.

"Dear Mary, As I lay my head on the pillow, I was enveloped

by my first dream (vision) for you. It was a feeling of extreme sexual frustration. My thoughts were, oh no, not now. This night is for Mary.

Then it came to me that this was how you must often feel, your physical need due to the loneliness this past year. The first vision of the night is usually something to let me know that I am in someone else's mind.

I made a note of the feeling on the pad beside my bed. Thank you for sharing that feeling with me. Pardon me if I'm laughing, but we need all the laughter we can get and this seemed like a bit of humor we could share.

Dream #1 - I fall back to sleep quickly and I enter a trailer park. The man on duty approaches me and says, "If you wish to buy or sell a trailer, I'm the guy to talk to." This is exactly what we need. In our conversation, he promises to teach us how to sell trailers. The balance of the dream has us showing and selling real estate. End of dream.

I note beside the written dream; perhaps you should try selling real estate, or do you? Perhaps this has spiritual meaning. It may be speaking of making a commitment to living God's plan for you. Actually, something clicked. This was a restatement of your question. I often get this in the first dream.

This man in the park of life could be reassuring you that you are ready to share what you know with others.

Dream #2 - Going back to sleep, I go on to dream again. This time I see you assigned to a government undercover job, investigating something.

In a tall building, we ride up the elevator and search different floors. We search rooms that people have slept in. We make beds and clean. We discourage non-essential people from knowing what we are doing.

We seem to be looking for a messy little girl. We find several false clues. We open a closet door and see a small replica of a room. It reminds me of a one-room dollhouse.

As we leave, we find a clue and follow a flower delivery truck. It is going to the address we need.

The flowers are delivered to the basement of a building. A mother is there with an altar or shrine she has constructed. She is willing to tell the story of the child she's lost. End of dream.

I wonder if you have ever thought of writing mystery stories? If this is from a spiritual level, it may represent the searching you are doing for a truth to help you get through each day.

Following the flower delivery truck reminds me of the saying to 'Take time to stop and smell the flowers'. You may need to find some way to bring fun into your life. It may be tending your garden, if you have one.

I would guess that your husband is worrying about your health and his spirit is trying to guide you. He needs you to get over these problems so that he can get on with his own spiritual journey.

The basement part of the dream may be telling you to get out of the basement of life. Get out and tell your story. Say, "I'm a widow." Stop protecting the child within yourself.

Dream #3 - You and your husband are in a restaurant being served pancakes and syrup. In a booth, both seated on the same side of the table, Buddy, a friend of mine, and his son join you. You are all given gold chains with money symbols hanging from them. You put your husband's chain around the hem of your straight beige, knit dress. You put your own chain around the waist of the dress.

Buddy gives you his and it becomes a lovely necklace. Your husband wonders about the gold chains. You are thrilled. The dream ends.

It was 6 A.M. when I opened my eyes. I sometimes wonder if my subject has to be asleep for me to dream for her. Writing down the final dream, I noted the fun you are having, can have. I noted the money symbols and gold chains. God seemed to be saying, "Relax, don't worry about the money."

I don't know if you have a Buddy in your life but I do. He's the kind of person who is always smiling. I met him in a store just a few days ago and he smiled as usual, all the time we talked. Another symbol of how happy you will be. Hope this helps. Vi

Mary wrote back. The answers she needed were in the dreams. She said she felt she'd been touched by her late husband, angels, and by God Himself.

"Dear Vi, There are eleven things in the dreams that are actually in my life. I'll underline the items for you as I write.

My husband and I own a trailer we used for a summer home in a trailer park. I will sell it now. It's been too painful for me to think about selling it before now.

I have often entertained the <u>thought of selling real estate</u> in my spare time. The idea of a government job was simply not in my picture until last week. I answered an ad in the paper for a research position. I was told it was detective type work for the U. S. Government. I'd be doing <u>research on people who owed FHA mortgage money</u>, thus '<u>looking under their beds</u>', etc.

The <u>search for the little girl could very likely be me</u>. When my husband died, I started an active search for myself as I had been as a little girl.

I've come to realize that I've always been very psychic and intuitive. I've always <u>tried to cover it up</u>, hide it from others.

Now I've decided to be honest with myself and with others about this.

When my husband was ill, I prayed for him, often, at <u>a shrine of my own</u>. As his health failed, I definitely became his caretaker in a most <u>motherly way.</u>

I've been in a <u>restaurant with him</u> many times and been <u>served pancakes and syrup</u>. I did have <u>a straight beige knit dress</u> and I wore it often. The part about the gold chains sounds good, definitely the future I'd like but certainly not representative of my present or my past.

You should know, the night you called I had just hung up from talking to the suicide hot line. You've given me reason to live."

A few weeks later, Mary attended a conference for writers. She met many women who also dreamed for inspiration and stayed with the group because she had always been interested in writing.

With this new outlook on life, her old job seemed more interesting and even easier. She stayed with it.

She ended the letter: "Thank you for our spiritual connection. Truly, angels touched us. Mary."

I always feel the presence of a higher power. I haven't the ability to give advice that would move someone to make changes in their lives the way these dreams do. The dreams paint pictures that make the person want to change. It never ceases to amaze me when the truths of other people's lives are made known to me in a dream. Either her higher spirit or, perhaps and, her husband had come through to help guide her. Because of the eleven underlined items, Mary's letter has become my favorite.

Chapter 18

Is He The Right Man?

In June, Ann asked, "I feel like it's time for a change. Can you dream for me?"

That night, short visions came fast and furiously. My feeling was that spirit had been trying to get her attention for a long time. The first vision was of the bell of a flower like a Lily of the Valley or a tulip, dangling head down, face to the ground. It was watching the bugs of life crawl by in the dirt. Could it be that she was higher than the life she was seeing. Could it be that she was like the caterpillar wanting to be a butterfly and all she had to do was look up. Her sense of unrest was why she asked her question.

The second vision was a ringing in my left ear. It reminded me of the saying to 'listen up!' The third was a view of building tops very much like the city she lives in. The fourth vision were words saying 'education is freedom' and 'a degree in nutrition was the way for her to go'. The fifth vision was a song. "Give me hope, help me cope, give me peace on earth."

The sixth vision was of a left hand reaching out for help. The seventh and final vision was another song. "Follow the yellow brick road." In other words, it was all hers if she would take the first step and get the education.

At 3 AM, I was exhausted! I took a sleeping pill thinking there must be enough here to get her started. In the letter I wrote her the next day I offered to dream again after she had taken some steps, moved forward based on what we'd seen in the visions.

By September, I had another letter from her sending me a love offering and asking for another dream. She was working on putting her life in a better order. All three of her children were now in school and she was going back to school also. She'd never thought of a career in nutrition but, since she had no other burning desire, she was going to look into this. She asked what I knew of the field. I did have a little experience to share.

However, her burning desire, this day, was knowledge of a man she had met. Was he the one for her? She gave me his name, Jack _____. I knew neither one of them and so this was truly up to spirit to advise and her to interpret, so I thought. However, a beautiful love story came through that was very much to the point.

The first dream is of a queen who is excited about doing a new thing. All she has to do is to push the button and review the last time she'd done it. Did I write a new thing? Maybe this 'before' time was in a past life.

This sounded to me that she'd been down this 'man' road before and was being told to think back. She is not a queen on a throne and should not expect things to be brought to her when she wanted them. But I kept these thoughts to myself because the answer was perfectly clear later.

I asked Spirit about the nutritionist job. In a vision I see headlines of American obesity; in the workplaces, in schools, and on the streets. There is a lot of need for people to teach us to eat right and if she should go into this, she can get by with minimal education or she can be a star in the field, based entirely on her efforts.

Then comes a song. "Take my hand, precious Lord, lead me on to the light, I am tired. I am weak. I am worn. Take me on through the night. Take me on to the light. Precious Lord, take my hand. Lead me on." I believe God is telling her to have faith, trust in Him to lead her.

Then another song comes. "If I had a hammer, I'd hammer in the morning. I'd hammer in the evening, all over this land. I'd hammer out danger. I'd hammer out a warning. I'd hammer out a love between a brother and a sister, all, all over this land."

If she took the advise of Spirit, this is what she'd be doing, hammering out a health warning to each person she met.

I asked Spirit, what about the new boyfriend, Jack? Would it help if I knew something about their relationship? Spirit answered that I didn't need to know.

Going back to sleep, I asked Spirit to tell me something about his looks. I was looking for verification or validation that would prove to Ann that I was in her realm. Words came. I didn't need to know.

While writing this on the paper, the thought came to me that this may be the answer. Ann didn't need to know anything about Jack. I left that up to her, for now.

Then the last dream came. It was a full-blown love story. A man and woman knew each other briefly. She went on to marry another. A busy highway separates their worlds. He rides his horse in the field on one side of the highway and watches for a glimpse of her in the field across the way. Years pass.

One day he sees her husband throwing away a wooden, spindle-backed chair. It crashes on the highway. Our man rushes to retrieve a leg. The rest gets pushed to the other side by the traffic. Soon, she comes riding up on the other side, looking for the chair. It obviously meant something to the two of them. A young boy, looking a lot like our man comes riding with her. She gets off her horse to pick up the pieces. All of the chair but one leg is there. She looks up to see him waving his arm, frantically, with that last piece in his hand. Their eyes lock and their thoughts are the same. "If only she'd waited for him." Then come the words, "Matches made in heaven are special".

I woke with a final song going through my head. "It's sad to belong to someone else when the right one comes along."

At the end of my letter to her, I couldn't help remark that if this man was the right one; she wouldn't have to consult a psychic.

As of this writing, there has been no response. Based on what you've read in the other people's lives, this has to say a lot for waiting.

Mice are symbolic
of poverty.

Chapter 19

Do I Call Her A Liar?

Elaine contacted me when it became clear to her that many things her mother-in-law had told her were downright lies. She, like Gail in a previous story, could not abide any dishonesty. Like Gail, after the dreams, she would be able to allow a gray area and still love the person involved.

Elaine lives in the south, her mother-in-law and a couple of her husbands' siblings and their families lived in a northern state. The mother was the only one she was in constant touch with. According to the mother, her other son's family was cold, rude, and greedy. Elaine was shocked by the tales of mental abuse this poor lady suffered, to the point that contact with the rest of the family was definitely cool.

Then a nephew moved south to attend a college nearby and they got acquainted. Elaine learned the truth was a lot different than what she'd been led to believe. The young man gave dates and events where all were together and had good times. These were dates and events when mother had said she was left at home alone.

The woman was going to be staying with Elaine for a few days and Elaine's instinct was to confront her about the lies. Needless to say, Elaine was totally upset.

In dream number one I see her going through a maze of rooms, the floors are filled with snapping alligators. Her concern, in the dream, is for the rest of her group as well as for herself.

My thoughts were that this described how Elaine felt right now. So far, she thought she had escaped the alligators' jaws. What had the woman said about her? What might happen to the love the children had for their grandmother when they found out?

In dream number two I see her waiting in her daughters' place of business. The lobby is being remodeled. She reads a brochure that is similar to her own. There is a wide ledge (or trough) around the

117

room, about four feet from the ceiling that seems filled with mice. A German Sheperd dog runs around the top of the trough, chasing a mouse. All of a sudden, the dog knocks the mouse out of the trough and onto the back of my neck. (It was so real. I jumped out of bed, turned on the light, and looked for something. Nothing was there. I had been lying on my back!)

Mice, to me, are symbolic of poverty. Perhaps the mother-in-law thinks of herself in this class, as actually poor or, poor me, they don't do enough for me. Her higher self, the German Shepherd dog is trying to make things happen to get her out of her rut or trough. This is a good example of the tug of war that goes on between one's ego (what we think) and our unconscious. The part of the remodeled lobby and business show her potential. Only she can remodel her life.

In dream number three, I'm cooking Christmas dinner for a crowd. No one helps. It is plain old potatoes with gravy, green beans from cans and dried out pot roast. There are no tables set up, no dishes set, and everyone waits for me to do everything. I'm slow. Some leave without saying anything. Someone asks, "Where are the grapes I always have in my potatoes?"

Elaine realized this was how her mother-in-law, perhaps, was seeing things. Perhaps she has a feeling of not being good enough to do the job she feels she has to do, according to other people. Perhaps she's not felt good enough to do any job, ever. Insecurity can drive a person to do and say strange things. Perhaps she no longer has the energy to do what she thinks others want of her.

Elaine's anger cooled, realizing there were things about this woman she didn't know. The visit came, was very enjoyable and on the last day Elaine confronted her with the truths she's learned, the lies she'd been told, and how she's finally become closer to the rest of the family. The mother-in-law laughed it off as probably being her 'other' self that day that told the lies. You can't change other people, you can only change how you think about them and deal with them.

Chapter 20

How Do I Get Judy To Marry Me?

This dream experience holds a good example of a person's essence. Your essence is one way I know I'm with you as my head hits the pillow. It can come as a vision, a smell, something I hear, or it can be a pain. Frank came through as an angry bear.

When Frank first entered my life he was 32 years old. This was the first of many phone conversations after we met during a Parents Without Partners meeting where I gave a speech.

"Vi, I went to a psychic a few weeks ago for help. She came up with the middle name of my friend Judy's daughter. I know that means we're supposed to be together, but Judy won't marry me. Will you dream for me? Perhaps it will tell me how to convince her," He had a quest.

"How close are you and Judy?" I asked.

"We dated for over a year, but we broke it off last February. We've been on-again, off-again ever since. We have a great time together and I know Judy wants to be with me. I can't understand our relationship. Is it or isn't it?"

"That seems like a reasonable question," I replied. "Tell me a little about yourself."

"My wife died a few years ago. I have our two boys, and things are tough right now. I'm between jobs."

"Do you have a trade?" I asked.

"No, not really," he quickly changed the subject, "Judy won't call me if I leave it up to her. She says she wants to date others. She says she doesn't love me. I know in my heart that she's right for me. I'd like a commitment. Is there anything you can tell me to help me convince her?"

119

"I can dream for you," I told him, "We'll put it in God's hands and see if He wants you two together."

"Oh, I'm sure of the answer," Frank said.

"God doesn't always see things the way we want Him to", I explained. "He might have something else for you to work on before you get the reward of this relationship."

Frank replied, "The psychic told me dates and names. I'm sure this is right for me."

I know psychics give some amazing information, but I was beginning to doubt Frank's interpretation of this particular information.

As I lay my head on the pillow that night, a pain shot through the toes of my right foot. "Ow!" I actually jumped and twisted to hold my toes. A vision of an angry bear with a thorn in his foot came to mind.

The pain subsided. I lay back only to be assaulted again. This time the pain, not as intense, was in the other foot.

Thinking of that angry bear, I knew if we could just get that thorn out, he would be a big old lovable bear once more. This was Frank's essence and there was hope for him. I drifted off to sleep.

In the first dream Frank and a guide are going somewhere. A large furniture store is in the way. Frank follows his guide through the store, never looking right or left.

However, his guide spots the owner of the store. The owner is a famous person and sits in a comfortable chair on a platform. The guide asks the famous person, "Why has this store full of luxury items been put in Frank's path?" And the dream ended.

Early the next morning Frank called. I'd only had the two messages this time. Frank disagreed with my theory of his essence.

"The pain in the toes is the pain I was going through when my wife died," he said, "I got rid of that pain when I joined Parents Without Partners. I met Judy there."

My belief that the subject always interprets best was a bit shaken as I agreed to accept his interpretation. Experience has taught me that ones' essence vision refers to the present, his anger now, not the past, the passing of his wife.

I continued, "The dream shows there is more to life than you see. You are walking through a great furniture store and not seeing the furniture. You have a single-minded attitude, to get out the other door."

"The store simply represents Judy's lifestyle," he came back. "She likes and owns nice things while I couldn't care less about them."

Frank decided we were seeing Judy's perspective. The furniture was important to her.

He said, "The dream, in the furniture store, was simply a replay of a phone conversation I had with Judy last night. She is used to nice furniture. She was the guide in the furniture store. She had been pointing out the difference in our taste in furniture over the phone. (Amazing! I picked up a phone conversation.)

He had told her, "Fancy furniture is not important to me. I know that I can't provide those things for her. She's used to luxury. I really believe she needs to move beyond material things and find love for me,"

"Frank," I made him pause. "Try putting yourself in the role of the other dream characters," I felt that he had missed an important point. "A furniture store needs furniture to be in business, to make money. You need to learn to make money. In the dream, you're not interested in anything around you. In your single-mindedness, you are marching straight through, missing the important person there."

I continued, "Important people, authority figures, often represent an authority higher than yourself. You need to open your eyes to something."

"Vi," Frank patiently told me. "You haven't told me anything new. Other people have told me the same things. I do believe you were in my subconscious. Can't you dream again for me and find something I can tell Judy to convince her to move in with me?"

I tried to change the subject, approach from another line of attack. "Frank, have you ever tried asking, 'Why am I suffering so much?' rather than 'How do I get Judy into my life?'"

His answer, "No, I'm fine."

"Okay, we'll try again tonight," I conceded.

In dream number two, a woman and two little boys are traveling through Mexico. They walk through the deserted center of a forgotten city. The streets are all paved and lined with large buildings.

"There's a lot to see and learn from the people who used to live here," she tells the boys.

Everything is very ornate, with curly wrought iron trimmings.

Spanish tiles are on the walls everywhere. They go in and out of buildings and down stairs into living quarters of the people who used to live there. The boys ask about everything.

Soon they are walking across the flat, endless desert. On the horizon they can see fast moving trains spewing billows of smoke into the sky.

It is a fascinating, exciting, and beautiful site to see. They walk closer in the hot sun. The trains become bigger. They pass first in one direction, then the other.

Mother cautions, "Don't get too close," They step onto the tracks anyway and then step back.

She says, "Wait until the next train passes, if you want to see one up close," The train rumble gets louder and louder. Toot, toot! The family steps back. When they turn to step back they see an empty dwelling and go to investigate. The trains are forgotten. They go inside and down the inevitable wrought-iron stairs leading to tiled walls underground.

The boys say, "This would be a place to live," All desire to go across the tracks or aboard the trains is forgotten. That is the end of the dream.

My intuition told me that Judy wanted no part of this guy. Maybe I could get him off Judy's back by telling him to move to Mexico. This dream seemed like a search for a better life.

He called early the next morning, again.

"Frank," I said, after relating the dream. "Look at this Mexico dream. You see beauty all around you (similar to the furniture store). You can't understand why no one lives there. It's beautiful but you still go underground."

I continue, "Could the empty buildings represent your empty relationship? Will you be exploring other empty relationships? Are you looking for the wrong thing in life? Perhaps you should consider a radical change in your life, perhaps a move to Mexico."

I thought I was doing really well. Then he shot me down.

"The dream was about Mexico because I used to live near the border. I've been there a lot and wouldn't go back," Frank said and continued, "I see Judy's concern about raising my two boys in this dream. We talked again last night on the phone and that was part of our conversation," he told me. "She's afraid they won't listen to her.

She worries about being responsible for their safety."

"Okay, but look at the symbolism," I replied. "In the dream the characters didn't stay in town because of empty useless beauty. They go out onto a hot, dry desert with blowing sand (a worse place to be) to find something else. The desert seems as endless as your trip through life can be, unless you solve your basic problem. The trains are a symbol of where you should be. Excitement and living beings are aboard them. Trains are symbolic of our journey through life. Trains take money to ride on. You look at the other people taking a journey on the trains but you turn your back."

"Try turning in a new direction," I suggested. "If you don't know which direction, ask for another dream. God will put opportunities in your life. The Bible says, ask and you shall receive. The problem will be solved for you."

"Frank," I said, "I find it interesting that you keep going underground to find living spaces. It is almost as if you have an unconscious wish to hide from life. That doesn't work. You have been moving across a dry space for a long time. You go underground again. The word 'again' is important. You told me your relationship with Judy is an 'on-again' relationship. Could this relationship be an empty underground place for you? Underground is not the way to move ahead."

He wasn't buying. He said, "Vi, I've got to have Judy in my life to feel complete. Please ask one more time for me."

"There are other ways to get an answer," I told him. "Some you can do yourself. Sit in meditation or simply daydream a story where you come up from a dark hole in the Mexican ground and see the sunlight. Jump on a train. See where it takes you,"

I added, "Think about it again as you go to bed at night. See it happening. The desert is endless, the holes dark. See yourself moving out into the light. This is a way to take charge of your life. Mom is also a higher authority, just like in the furniture dream. She seems to offer a chance to get on the right track. Someone on the other side, a relative or guardian angel, is waiting to get you on the right track."

We talked professions, mostly photography. We had both done some darkroom work. He seemed to know more about the darkroom than I. He admitted to having dropped the interest. After telling him I had sold my photos, he seemed to have a renewed interest. If he made this decision, I would be glad to dream again for him. Perhaps photography was to be his profession.

However, he was adamant I try the dream process, about Judy, again. "Okay," I said. "I've never dreamed so many times for the same person on the same question before. I don't know if it will work, but I'll try again."

My dreams that night were definitely for Frank. I even gave the dream a title, 'Moving Judy'!

In dream number three it is moving day. We wait outside for the movers. Their truck comes barreling down the street, sliding sideways to a stop. I am furious.

"You could have killed us all!" I shout at the driver. "This is a 30 MPH zone."

We all share an instant dislike for the driver. We are a woman, a man, and some children.

"I have to call back to the office, let them know I'm here," The driver ignores our anger. He has a cellular phone but doesn't know how to use it.

"Will you help me dial?" he asks. I take the phone and punch in the numbers.

He is close to me. His fingers are all yellow from smoking and his breath smells badly.

He lies on the phone, "If the other truck driver hadn't messed up, I wouldn't have been late," The second truck driver would be in trouble now.

"Get going! Everyone! We'll be moved out today!" I yell. I let my anger for him wash over everyone.

The second driver arrives. He is very nice. I slip him my business card. "Call me if you have any problems over this incident," I whisper to him.

There is reason to fear the first driver.

I return to the business at hand. I find the screwdriver on the mantle and I proceed to unscrew all the switch plates in the house to take with me to put in my new home. The dream ends.

As I contemplated this dream, it occurred to me that I might be getting a description of Frank in this first driver. It's probably a good thing we had only spoken by phone. He might think I was passing judgment on him. As I went back to sleep I received another dream.

Dream number four showed me an extremely poor family. The husband shouts from a back step to his wife to get his friend a beer. She's in a small, poorly equipped kitchen and moves around as though half asleep. The dream ends.

I typed all the dreams and my interpretations and sent them off in a letter to Frank. Maybe reading the written words would allow him to see more clearly. It was obvious to me that this was the life Judy feared.

I didn't answer my phone that day. Frank's obsession bothered me. Part of my letter to him was:

"Put yourself in truck driver #1's place. Was he only thinking of himself? Are you thinking only of yourself in your relationship with Judy? Are her needs different than yours? Perhaps your own needs are not what you think they are. Are you forcing something?

Put yourself in truck driver #2's place. You are about to become a victim. Are you setting yourself up to be hurt again? The woman in the story realizes he's in trouble. She's willing to help him.

Could this explain Judy's soft spot for you? Simple pity? Pity over what? The death of your wife? Perhaps she senses you're headed for more trouble and is tempted to help you.

If this relationship is meant to be, she'll be there a year from now, or five years from now.

Driver #1 cannot see the numbers or sequence. If you are tied together by the number or names the psychic gave you, you will still be tied together in the future.

Isn't it interesting that in this dream you have trouble seeing the phone, in another dream you don't stick around to see the train and in the first, you didn't see the furniture?

I believe God is telling you to work on other problems now. Is there something in your life you refuse to look at? Is this why your relationship is so important to you? Does it keep you from tackling your real problem?

Put yourself in the position of the truck. You are almost out of control. Someone else is driving your life, very recklessly. You must only go 30 MPH in a 30 MPH zone.

Frank, my last dream is a vision of your future if you stay on your current path. It is not a nice picture for Judy. My hope is that you will put your relationship with her aside for now. Find out what you should be doing to earn money."

After receiving my letter, Frank called. He believed that God spoke to us in dreams. He knew that I had reached a level of consciousness beyond us. Still, "Vi, you didn't tell me anything new," Frank said. "Many other people have told me the same things," Those "other" people knew him, I didn't.

Frank had analyzed the dreams completely. His version was that it was all a replay of his life.

"I need Judy in my life to feel complete. The last vision is from her mind. She thinks this is the way we will live. The kitchen I have now is old and kind of torn up.

"The moving day dream," he said, "is something I arranged for her recently. She liked two of the movers but disliked the third, immensely.

"Then, we had to change all the switch plates in her new apartment. This is a prime example of her expensive tastes." He continued to take the dreams matter-of-factly. I was astounded at how much of their lives I had seen.

Frank saw only what he wanted to see. Nothing in the dreams told him he would have Judy and be happy. He wanted to ignore the dreams, change them around.

The phone calls from Frank suddenly stopped about three weeks after our first contact. I was really concerned about his single-minded attitude. I went so far as to suggest he get professional counseling, which may have been why he stopped calling.

Six years later, he returned my phone request for an update on his life. Nothing had changed. He'd been through two similar relationships since Judy. He was going, that day, to apply for a maintenance position at a factory near his home.

Six more years into his life and he still had not done anything about a trade. If he had just accepted the hand God extended him in these dreams, we might have seen another story of great gifts through dreaming.

Chapter 21

Know When To Walk Away

Marie, a mother and grandmother, fussed about her relationship with her daughter-in-law. They'd known each other for years but were barely talking. Marie was afraid to say anything for fear of causing trouble in the family, for fear of not seeing her grandchildren.

She asked for word from God as to how to improve this relationship.

The first vision I have that night is of being surrounded by pitch black. Then I notice a small light far off in a distance. This is hard to believe so I opened my eyes to see if anything was penetrating my eyelids. Nothing was. It was a dream vision. This first vision is usually the dream subject's essence so I wondered if this was how she felt about this situation? Did her subconscious see the solution as a distant possibility?

The next vision is also black. Gradually lines appear like bare tree trunks and branches. I am looking at a dead forest. The prognosis for this relationship does not look good. Then the lines became the outline of five heads and shoulders. A light line snakes around connecting each one. I hear the words 'Queenship Mary.' I know they are figureheads.

Marie filled me in later that this was her immediate family. I had no idea. There are five of them and the drawing I did even resembled their sizes.

Then came the first dream. In the dream, Marie drives her daily route going out of her way to drive through a hospital to pick up three friends. They are neither sick nor working there. She'd left an opportunity to be with her husband to do her route. On arriving this day she finds none of them waiting; no message either. She has trouble driving out of the hospital area, everything has changed. No one told her. She gets out of her car and gets into an experimental vehicle built to travel through the hospital. The trouble really begins.

She speeds out of control, goes into wrong areas, etc. All this time she could have been with her husband. She stops and asks several times for her friends, but no luck.

What I saw in this dream story was the futility of trying to build a relationship with this daughter-in-law. I saw how things could get more out of control and I also saw an important person she was leaving behind, her husband. She agreed this was about how things were going.

In dream number two, I'm setting up a sound system, microphone, music stand, and preparing to sing. The words come, "Come with me. It's somewhere in your heart."

Marie and I met in church and she does sing.

In dream number three I'm in the back room of a church with friends. A line of black performers is in the sanctuary, up front, on stage. My group slips in to hear. We see an empty row of seats in the front and take them. One of the performers orders us out of those seats. They are reserved for them. We find another row and sit. The same performer orders us out of those also. We hear her say, "Those darn white people!"

Unknown to me, Marie had been to see "The Coasters" perform the night before I dreamed for her. Her group of people had changed seats twice and an usher was sent to stop them. Picking up on what they'd done the night before was verification that I was in her realm.

I thought my night of dreaming for her was over as it was six A.M. I hadn't gotten much. I turned out the light and thoughts of another person's message came. My mind went over the message and wouldn't leave it until I realized it might also be for Marie and wrote it down. The message was about spiritual growth.

This other person, Joy, is a Christian psychic. Joy was frustrated because she could not do the things John Edwards and James Van Prague do, bringing back the spirits of loved ones passed and healing the rifts left in the wake of death. The message for Joy and Marie, and myself, is that ours is the greater service. On TV, John and James build bridges of belief. Not meaning to minimize the wonderful work they do, the message is that a lot more needs to be done after that. We can lead people to their personal spirituality, help them find their purpose in life and heal other wounds they may have and show the way of an entire life lived in communication with Father God.

I wondered if this is a glimpse of Marie's path?

I still hoped to get an answer about the original question about the daughter-in-law. It came to me that the answer, or problem, lies in the daughter-in-law's childhood. It's something Marie cannot heal. While chasing her friends in the hospital dream, she's trying to do the right thing or what society might expect of her. It takes place in a hospital because it's part of society's ills. Marie gets lost in life's twists and turns and looses track of an important thing (the work shown in Joy's message) symbolized by her husband or male side in dream number one.

Dream number two, the singing, is a talent God gave Marie and she must use it as much as possible.

Dream number three may go back to Marie's daughter-in-law's attitude. She is just a performer on the stage of Marie's life. Marie should take whatever seat she wants and simply watch. It doesn't matter. Marie can't change the performance.

I told Marie that sometimes, when I write my own dreams, one word will stand out and I'll forget the entire rest of the action as meaningless. This one word will hold the key to the message. Words I picked out as possibilities are travel, hospital, experimental, choice, move, route (path?). Then I had to leave it with her. Several years later the situation with the daughter-in-law has not changed. The fact remains; I did see her out there that night on the town at a concert, changing seats. I was in her realm.

My thoughts were that
the floating tables
were musical notes.

Chapter 22

The Songwriter

Ted Jones (real name) is a member of the dream class I attend at the Haden Institute. He has dedicated his life to being a songwriter and works in Nashville. He plays and sings for us every time we have a meeting in North Carolina and we all agree that we are lucky to have him in our group. He's very talented.

One speaker this particular weekend, Diana McKendry, drew two triangles on the board. She said this first example was how most people view life. She wrote 'Do' at the top. She wrote, 'Be' on the bottom left corner and at the bottom right corner she wrote, 'Have.' In other words what we do will lead to who we are (or be) and that will lead to what we get (have or achieve). Diana said the truth was the top and first point was to 'Be.' 'Be' all that we were meant to be. The second corner, bottom left should be 'Have.' The last corner should be 'Do.' After we've found out who we really are, we'll acquire what we need and we can do more for the world.

Ted's question was "Am I doing or am I being?" In other words was he on the right path?

My first dream for Ted came with a title. It was "Thanksgiving Day." A companion and I take a seat at a floating table, one of two floating tables. We put up a flag to mark our spot and get up to get our food. We return with it to our table. An elderly, handicapped couple catch our attention and we try to help them get their plates of food and secure a table. The other table is taken but more floating tables appear as more people appear. We have to move quickly to secure a table for our elderly people.

My thoughts were that the floating tables were musical notes. When I drew a picture of what I'd seen, put a flag on our table, it looked very much like a musical note. Notes float in the air until you put them on paper. Then they float once again as they're sung as a song.

In the second dream, Ted is to exercise a horse by riding him. Inexperienced horse handlers bring out a very small horse. Ted gets on. It looks dumb to me. How could they bring him this horse? He is used to greater horses. He gets on and rides anyway.

My thoughts were that he has ridden many times before, meaning possibly he's written songs in past lifetimes and this is a road he must follow. He's destined for greater things.

Next dream is a vision of a hand holding several sheets of sheet music. My thoughts were that surely he is on the right path.

Then a song invaded my senses and would not leave until I wrote the words down. It was the country song "Crazy." My thoughts were along the lines that perhaps Ted was crazy for devoting his life to this. Then upon examining the song I realized that the person singing was not crazy but knew exactly what he wanted.

I wrote this out and gave it to Ted. The synchronicity was that, unknown to me, Ted is an avid horse rider. He also has a special fondness for elderly people. A couple days after getting home I received a post card from Ted. He wrote "Thank you again for dreaming for me. It was truly a marvelous experience. I had some doubts, but you have made me a believer."

Chapter 23

Which Path Should I Follow

I met Cat, also, at a Dream Intensive put on by the Haden Institute. The last day, as we said our final prayers, she gave an emotional plea for someone unknown to me. Tears were in her eyes. Before we went home she asked me to dream for her.

Her question: Professionally, should I do the training to be a presenter? Should I continue to see children? (She is a therapist.)

My prayer to God that night as I lay my head on my pillow was to, please, wipe clean my own thoughts of the day and give me an answer for Cat.

In vision #1: I am up on a step stool about to clean a ceiling fan. I spin it slowly hitting all four blades with a cleaner like Windex in preparation of cleaning them.

Note: My husband does our blade cleaning and cleans one at a time. So this cleaning all at once seems quicker, more efficient.

In the first dream I stand with others on the edge of a new community. (This could be the Haden Institute work.) We go to a large furniture warehouse where we all point out the furniture we want. My focus is on bookcases or large wall units of some kind. (My thoughts are that we each are going to take away different yet similar things, the furniture, from this course. And they'll be part of our lives from now on.)

In dream number two the male in my house suddenly jumps up and says, "I hear a knocking." The dog doesn't bark so I know it is Spirit.

In dream number three I see a path that I travel several times a day. It goes along the beach beside the water. Suddenly beside me in the sand is a pocket of snakes. First one, and then two heads poke out of the hole. One of them hits me on a finger on my left hand. I hurry past them. Now I'm angry and call them vipers. Should I get medical attention?

In dream number four my husband is remodeling our living room. It is two stories tall. (Not at all like mine.) He is getting it ready to sell and seems frustrated that it hasn't. He's painted the first story very nicely but has just stuck sheets of metal and plywood on the second level to cover the walls. Our neighbor has a family member who yells all the time. A man is coming to view the house so I go outside. I meet the neighbor for the first time. His sick family member is laying on a board in the yard and still yelling. As I talk to the neighbor, his face changes before my eyes. His right cheek is growing larger. I realize he must have the same disease as the other, which I assume is autism. (I have no connection with this other than seeing one rarely on the street.) The neighbor wants to see the inside of my house while he has a chance. I arrange for someone to take him in but I lock up the dog myself. (I once had a bad experience when walking my dog through a group of loud people she didn't know and have kept her close to home ever since. I don't feel this has any bearing on the question.)

On telling Cat the dreams, the synchronicity comes clear. She tells me that the person she was so emotional about during prayer time was indeed autistic. I had no way of knowing. She agrees the new community could very well be the Haden Institute community. She has a chance to be part of the Haden Institute, a growing school for people interested in leading dream groups. Another synchronicity is that her living room has a two-story high ceiling and they are remodeling. I was in her realm.

The scene that held the most impact for her was the scene with the four bladed fan. That is how she feels after leaving a weekend at Haden Institute. She gets so immersed, she feels she must clean the blades off before returning home to normal life.

The message in the snake dream is based on Jungian Psychology and myths. The bite of the snake is to signify that spirit has already passed the wisdom you need into you. She had only to wait God's timing. In the dream she was on her way to the beach, the ocean, the spiritual side of life.

Chapter 24

Why Can't I Remember My Dreams?

Clarisa (she wanted to make sure I spell it with one 's') wanted to know why she doesn't dream anymore or why she can't remember her dreams?

Clarisa is a member of my dream group at home and usually has many dreams. The last dream she brought to the group for help in understanding concerned a lion chasing her through a dark tunnel. Her thought was to make it follow her and keep it away from her son and husband. End of dream.

After this dream, feeling it might predict trouble, Clarisa and her husband looked for a break from life. They went for a long road trip. They visited all the extended family and saw many parts of the country they'd not seen. He developed a cough on the trip and tired easily. Well, they were both getting older, she reasoned. When they got home it developed quickly into a serious illness and he died in the hospital a couple of weeks later. She now sees the lion in her dream as a warning about her husband's demise. She feared something like this for him, their son or herself when she brought the dream to the group.

Clarisa stopped coming to the dream group, stopped going anywhere, for several months. Her dreams also stopped. She wanted to hear from her husband and hoped coming back to the dream group would help her in remembering her dreams once more.

After her second time there, she shared the whole story of the dream and how she now knew it had been a death warning. One of her daughters had a dream about the same time that also foretold the death. Of course they didn't understand the dreams that way when they had them.

The dreams, the very happy trip that reunited them with family and friends they'd not seen for a long time, the short illness and the beautiful way this all seemed to have been brought together by a higher power brought them to believe it was simply his time. They were warned as a means of giving them strength. Now she wanted someone to dream for her and find out why her dreams had seemingly stopped.

In my dreams that night, I sit at a birthday table. Two little girls with big bushy hair full of ringlets sit with their back to a camera. It is a TV camera. One of the girls has just lit the candles on the cake. "Turn around," I ask, "so we can get your pretty faces in the picture." They won't turn. End of the dream.

My thoughts were that the girls represented part of Clarisa's unconscious that had, for a while, been hidden. Clarisa wanted her unconscious to open to her once more.

The next dream is just a feeling. I wake feeling very proud of those two girls. Knowing Clarisa has offered many wonderful insights to others concerning their dreams, I felt she needed this ability once more, right now, to gain back a sense of self-worth, pride and purpose.

In the next dream, the girls and I are in a room completely surrounded by glass walls that have a smoky haze to them. My thoughts are that we are coming out of the haze. The death had been a shock and was followed by many months of trying to find her way in life without her partner. She truly has been coming out of a haze.

In the last dream I only have to talk to the girls and they agree to turn around and become more public. My thoughts were that things are turning around for her and the dreams will come back. This readiness of the return of dreams had been mentioned at dream group and the other members of the group concurred. Sharing with us, would make it easier to dream.

When I met her the next morning at the community walking pool (purely by accident, but then again, is anything by accident?) I told her of the dreams. Her eyes widen with the first sentence. She has twin granddaughters with hair like I described and of a similar age. I didn't know. They were part of a birthday celebration just before her husband died. It was both Clarisa's birthday and the twin's birthday. The synchronicity was there. God brought us together on this one. Another synchronicity was that she had a hard time "going public" with the death of her husband. She had a hard time saying she was a widow. I didn't know this either.

She added the possibility that the twins signified two sides of herself, since everything in the dream is you. The two sides of her were the one who had a husband and the one who didn't.

To top it all off, the same night, she had a dream or visit (if you so believe) from the spirit of her husband. She was happy once more. In her dream, which she shared with the group, she was with her husband in a small familiar town in South America. He never spoke, just seemed to be showing her the way. They went down stairs from a two story building into an empty street. They walked around a corner and saw a second building; this one was one story but had a terrace on the roof with clothes drying on a line. She wanted to get the clothes down and tried to jump up to that level. Her husband stood on the stairs showing her the way. She then took the stairs. She grabbed tights or panty hose off the line and disgustedly threw them over the side of the roof, onto the now crowded street. They fell on the head of a familiar looking woman who was talking to her husband.

Our interpretation is that her husband is telling us in the dream that her life is changing. She's gone around a corner. The clothes could be her old way of looking at things. The tight, restrictive pantyhose was the period of mourning she'd been through. It was not for her anymore. She'd gone down into a valley (the street) and now back to the roof, higher in perspective, to throw away the clothes of her old persona.

She had no view of
her future herself,
at all.

Chapter 25

Divorces Effect On Children

Erma had recently begun attending the same church I do. She approached me with a request. Could I find out if she was on the right path in life? She had no view of her future, at all. I think we'll find out that is because her present was so busy.

First vision I have, as I lay my head on the pillow that night, is of construction in a housing development. I wonder how many people could live there? A voice said to count the golf balls under each step.

The next day Erma said I was seeing where they lived. It is a fairly new apartment complex and a lot of golfers live there.

The first dream has me studying a crime scene in some shallow water. It is in the dark of night. Using flashlights, I make notes on everything we find. It is a gruesome scene. I map the flow of the water in the stream and its tributaries. It is persistent, painstaking, dedicated work in which I have some pride. Coming closer, I see there is a body bag with two heads. Both mouths have narrow overbites causing their mouths to look unusual.

It took Erma some time to relate this dream story to her life. A breakthrough came several days later, as she was making notes for her lawyer about her upcoming divorce. The dream memory drifted back.

"This is what that crime scene is about," she thought, "My two children are the victims!"

God was telling her this was her first concern at this time in her life. We often have to clear up today's problems or, even, problems from our past before we can move ahead.

In a later dream that same night I'm at a gathering where some people get up and sing. I'm handed a note saying that it's time for me to sing, and now I'm sorry I volunteered. I have to perform, go through the motions. It's my turn.

This reminds me of another's dream that told a man that he

agreed to the terms when he bought the ticket. Is this high divorce rate something planned in the greater scale of things? Are our lessons coming faster?

The song I sing is, "There is a place where you can always go, come with me. It is a place where you can be yourself, come with me."

I felt the song was asking for more faith on her part. She'd gone to the gathering (the marriage perhaps) and now needed to get out. There is another place where she can grow and be herself.

Chapter 26

What Vocational Path Should I Follow?

Karen was ready for a change. She'd been doing psychotherapy for quite a while and was feeling burned out. Her needs seemed to be for continued growth; spiritually and emotionally. And you can't forget about financial.

In the first dream I had for her I enter a room from long ago. Just inside a very ornate front door sits a man, a storyteller. He has on a strange costume (quilted, gold cape, hat, cane, puffy long pants and sleeves). His hair is long and his face has a perky little beard. A woman comes in the door to inform him of something. He tells her to take care of it herself and turns back to us to finish his story.

My thoughts were that the storyteller represented the story deep in each of us and also in each of her clients. She's not giving him time to entertain her, or finish the story. If she was the woman who got shoved aside, perhaps this was how she was feeling. Maybe she was putting herself last, thus causing a burn out. A vacation plus some faith she was doing the right thing is needed.

The next dream begins as a black background with brilliant blue swirls. I wonder, is this the mist of her dreams? Then it changes into a black room with many TV screens on the walls. Each screen holds a different action. Barely visible are three people sitting in the center, low to the scene, discussing what they see.

The first synchronicity is here. This reminded Karen of a TV studio she'd recently been in, discussing a show about dreams. I knew nothing of this part of her life.

In the next dream I'm leaning over a table under a light doing something with my hands. Although a heater clicks on loudly, like a zipper being zipped up, I am so engrossed I don't react. A voice says,

"This is for the spirits!"

This is where the second synchronicity comes in. Karen was making jewelry in her spare time and being quite successful with it. This is a talent she should pursue. It is for the spirits, more pointedly, her spirit.

Then a voice says, "Boy, is your in-box full!" I asked her if she'd been writing her dreams. She said no. Her inbox probably was full and spirit had a lot to tell her.

Next comes a song, "Let the mountains tremble, let the waters part. Let the hand of fate stir a troubled heart." To me this is saying, be patient.

The next dream comes and it is only midnight. The thought went through my mind that her inbox must indeed be full. In the dream I see a squirrel working a nut. Dollars drop out of the shell. He flits away jumping from tree to tree. There is often some point in a dream when sense, as we know it, dissolves. This dream has two such points, the second being that the squirrel has a big feather. I haven't a clue except she may be doing too much, jumping from tree to tree instead of working that one nut that held the money. If she is the feather, there may be some situation in her life where she feels completely out of place, like the feather on a squirrels back, or maybe like she is about to be dropped.

There were two more rather involved dreams that night for her. Her inbox was indeed full.

Chapter 27

Robert Van De Castle, Ph.D.
Author of "Our Dreaming Mind"

I read this book in 1995 and was thrilled to have all this information at my fingertips. The book includes a history of dreams, who does it, how long has this been going on, who's researching it today, what research is going on, what inventions have been credited to dreams, how different cultures have used and do use dreams, and how various religions view dreams. I had to tell the author of my own experiences and I was able to track him down.

On hearing my story, he asked me to dream for him. He asked me to contact his angels for him.

In the first dream for Bob, I pass a house that has old furniture for sale in the yard, two chairs and a settee. They look super old but on closer inspection I see they have been restored with a shiny varnish. They are actually good sturdy furniture. I ask the owners to save them for me until evening. The price is $500.00.

This gives me a chance to think it over. They are willing because they say they know my daughter.

In the dream, in the conversation with the people selling the furniture, I learn their house is also for sale. It is small and full of history. It's next to a canal or entrance to a harbor. It has two main rooms. A lot of people are around outside and I see a couple fall down a sand hill. Walking around the outside I see what appears to be a third room that runs the length of the house. I see cobblestone.

Still in the dream, I'm torn. I love the history, the canal and the many people. I realize antiques are lined up to be sold. My mind floats in a different direction. Can I get my original pieces any cheaper?

A second dream comes. It has my mother worrying about my

physical safety and the lack of a restaurant. Things mothers worry about. Indecision, indecision. Was Mom one of his angels that we contacted?

More memory comes to me about the house. There seem to be many ballrooms and many people are going in and out swinging doors. I know they are toilet areas.

Talking to Bob on the phone, I found out that he was going through a period of indecision.

I was not about to point out the symbolic meanings I saw. He has done a lot of research, himself, in the area of dreaming for others. Other researchers are using a ceremony he devised. People gather in a group, choose a subject, and dream for that person.

One symbol that struck me was the toilets where you get rid of old attitudes. Another was the emphasis on antique furniture, things of the past and getting rid of them also.

He was surprised that I got a description of the temporary place he was currently living. That's why all the detail about this house. His angels wanted to make sure he knew of our connection. At least one good thing came of this, for me. Robert Van de Castle autographed a copy of his book and sent it to me.

Chapter 28

Henry Reed
Author of "Dream Medicine"

Henry is a long time dream researcher, one of the regular writers for the Edgar Cayce group, A.R.E. in Virginia Beach. He's the author of Dream Medicine: Learning How To Get Help From Our Dreams. He contacted me after reading an article I had published in Dream Network Magazine. My article was on dreaming for others and he asked me to dream for him.

In the first dream we seem to be testing his knowledge of dream symbols. We start at one and stop at five, our first correction. Five is to talk, share, and let your feelings out. My thoughts, on waking and reading my notes, were that this is good advice for both of us. Little did I know at that time that five was also the number of dreams I would have for him this night.

In dream two we go into a theater for a church service. I sit next to someone I know and newspapers are passed out wherein the words to the songs are written. I leave in my friend's car. A big Hollywood star also gets in with us and hands my friend a special plant as though someone gave it to him and he didn't want it. After we drop him off, we stop at another friend's home to get advice on keeping the plant alive. We are jittery and laugh a lot. I expect my friend to name who gave it to her but she doesn't. When I'm alone with the plant expert I tell and find some truth. There is a history between these people of which I wasn't aware.

My interpretation: The plant, for me, is something I've been given to nurture, keep alive. For me, that's my dream work as I'm sure it is also for Henry. The plant is healthy and growing when we received it. We turn to experts for how to give it the best care, but we must do the work ourselves. The unknown history between Henry and myself is probably the fact that books by and about Edgar Cayce were my first, and for a long time, my main source of knowledge about dreams. I read Henry's columns in the *Venture Inward Magazine* (a publication about Edgar Cayce) for years and his other newsletter, *The Sundance Journal.*

At one time, frustrated by the information I was collecting from people I dreamed for, feeling someone should know about this proof of communication between people in their dreams, I sent it off to the experts. I just sent the whole thing to someone in the Cayce organization (could have been to Henry) and never had any response from them. In my naiveté, I probably didn't think to include my address.

So, as evidenced by the dream, they had helped nurture my dreaming for others and there is a history between us of which they are not aware. The church in the theater part, I interpreted as pointing out the sacredness of the subject.

In dream number three I'm alone again. I go to a restaurant, take a ticket and agree to a beer with my food (something I never do). I tell someone at my table about a star giving my friend the plant. That person also knew of the history between them.

Vision number 1: I see my hand drawing something. I start at the bottom and go up in what ends up looking very much like the outline of a basketball court. End of the vision

Wondering what path the meaning of the dream would take if I drew it, on waking I did draw it. I then realize I have drawn a Mandela. Henry is well known for these and had promised me one. I am the one being given the image of the Mandela. Could it be that Henry and I are at opposite ends of the basketball court, each waiting for the ball to enter our courts?

In dream number 4, I go to church and dinner at the church. An old minister holds forth on his wife's accomplishments. I am fascinated because I seem to know something others do not.

In the fifth dream, I cross a street and begin a popular walk that climbs a hill. People pass me, then turn and offer to let me go first. I decline. There are two ways to go. I've never been this way before and I tell them I'm taking my time. I then choose the one that goes straight uphill. I step over tree roots that hold the hill together. I stop and look back, marveling at the view.

I'll let Henry tell you what he found in these dreams that pertained to him.

"Dear Carol, When I first read the dreams I knew right away that your dreams weren't random; however, I could also tell that they were not at a literal level, and would take some time to explore for their meaning. For now, I'll tell you about the literal level.

I believe that many people can dream for other people, maybe even most, but I'm more interested in how dreams apply, and the relationship between the value of the dreams for you and the value for the other person. Most people have difficulty understanding how a dream can apply in both directions (the dreamer, the other person "dreamed for") but my assumption is that it is always/usually that way."

Henry continued, "Going into a theater for a church service. I responded immediately to this image, as for many years (but less so in the past few years) I have wanted to create a spiritual event that would be like a theater for people to watch/participate in. I used to spend a lot of time thinking about how it might go. At first it was with dreams, I envisioned a ceremony taking place on stage, where dreams would be blessed, and then people would bring their theater ticket up to the dream shrine to have it energized and take home to put under their pillow for a special dream. Later, as I moved from what dreams taught me into other areas of spiritual experience, my thoughts for how to combine spirituality and theater broadened out, but became less definite. Having this theme appear in your dreams suggests to me this desire is still active within me, as if it is unfinished business."

(This is one of those synchronicities, an actual fact of his life I would not know being shown me.)

"Keeping the special plant alive fits into this long-standing theme. Years ago, when I published the Sundance Dream Journals, one of the dreamers who dreamed for the journal and its implications for society, had a dream in which a UFO came to land on the earth. It was a female deity who held out for us a special plant.

"The idea that God speaks to us in dreams is as old as the Bible, so people will not be shocked by your revelation. I have the distinction of being someone that someone else wrote about, a psychiatrist who believed as you do that God speaks in dreams, even today, and wrote that I had proven that with my "dream tent" work back in the early 70's. There is a sense with me that this original dream work which I kind of abandoned, still calls to me, and that I should return to it, to offer the 'dream tent' to others."

"A history between these people," could refer to the folks who got enthusiastic about the Sundance Dream Journals and their prophecies.

"The truth coming out (in the dream) resonates with what I've been thinking for some time, I need to come out with a book that is not Cayce related, but expresses my ideas. The issue is a more practical one."

Henry wrote about Dream 2, "Dream 2: Never drinking beer … I am a recovering alcoholic. Dreams came in to replace the alcohol. 'Recovery' is a part of my dream work; in a lot of dimensions." (Another synchronicity.)

On the third dream, back at church, Henry writes, "I guess I'm the old minister. My wife is interested in the same ministry as me but doesn't have the recognition, and so I promote her some." (Another synchronicity.)

The fourth dream going up the hill, Henry writes, "On the popular walk up a hill, taking my time. I'm sure taking my time getting around to that book … (Henry since has published his book DREAM MEDICINE: Learning How To Get Help From Our Dreams).

Henry ends, "Again, thanks for traveling with me so far on this. Henry Reed"

Chapter 29

Robert Hoss
Author Of "Dream Language:
Self Discovery Through Imagery And Color

Robert asked for a dream for his daughter. Out of several dreams only one rang true, according to his daughter. In the middle of the dreams was a vision of a hand holding a tray of shells and candles. Another hand reached up and moved the candles aside to make room for one more. His daughter was about to give birth.

Once before I dreamed for a woman who was worried about a son she'd not seen for a long time. The dreams essentially told her to let go. He was on his own path and deserved to learn his own lessons.

In another instance, a man worried me, a handicapped man, who'd befriended my grandson. I asked for information about him and saw him on a riding lawn mower going around in circles on a paved parking lot. In other words, he was no threat. He was harmless, not even able to cut grass.

I've long held the impression that I needed permission to dream for someone, permission to dip into their world. I can learn what they mean to me, or to the person asking, but not anything else unless they give me permission.

He asks why I hang out
with the dishwasher
all the time.

Chapter 30

Dreaming For Groups

Having said I would find blocks in my way if you asked me to dream about what your adult child or a neighbor were doing, I have had some success when dreaming for groups of people. The requester needs to be a part of that group.

The first dream experience like this was a small retail store that specialized in metaphysical items. They asked me to dream about the future of their business. I expected two people the day I went to deliver the dreams, but there were four. They put a closed sign on the door and took me into a back room to read the dreams to them. The dreams, given the subject, made no sense to me. In the dreams I see a conspiracy going on with people meeting under the stairs and behind buildings at night.

Not a word was said when I finished reading. No questions. There were other dreams but they seemed anti-climatic after this opening sentence. It was strange.

The people thanked me and ushered me out the door. I was a little miffed. I treasure the feedback, the things in their lives I see that I have no way of knowing. At least I deserve a free used book. They had many. This bothered me for a week until I went back to the store under the pretense of buying something. There was an out of business sign on the door. End of group.

A lady named Carol contacted me via e-mail for a dream about her dream group. How neat!

In the first dream, I travel across a bay to a big city to do our dream theater. Then I'm traveling back across the bridge to go home. Our children, whom we've missed greatly, meet us and travel across the bay with us. One sister gets presents. It's her birthday.

Carol wrote back that their dream group has a guru. She's also an actress and the area they live in is like the area the dreams described.   They've been talking about investing in a young artist community to be located on River Road.   Thus the dream theater and going across the bridge.   The day before the dream, Carol had been sending out emails to her daughter-in-law, as it was her birthday.   She also belongs to this dream group that she now labels as a lucid dreaming group and says her relationship with this daughter-in-law is more like being sisters.

Dream two included my grandson.   It seemed to be a continuation of the first dream.   He has something he wants to tell me. He is happy to report that he has had his first sexual encounter. He is now a man and proud of it. He is determined to do better with his life, as he is about to be a father. The girl (did I notice the dark haired, blue mini-dragon in the group?) She's the one. I'm shocked. Not that he had sex, but what will the child look like? I ask, "Are you sure it isn't someone else's baby?" He's sure.

Carol writes back about this one that she has a grandson in his second year of college and he does have a girlfriend. She hopes this is not literal for at least a few more years.

The dragon! Her daughter-in-law had been having some intense dreams about blue dragons and white tigers. Carol had gone to bed, programming her mind for a specific dream saying to herself, 'the sky is filled with flying blue dragons, not evil but of a fierce nature.' A stuffed blue dragon has become a mascot for their group. She believes the sex part is saying this project of hers is coming of age, has gained its' man-hood status. It is making a connection that will give birth to new life, new opportunities.

The next vision I have is of a bumper sticker I saw at a dream conference, "I love my country but I think it's time we start seeing other people." Carol said she had been trying to get a message about peace on her own. Another bit of synchronicity.

I write: I don't think I'm sick (I often pick up on the health or emotions of the dream subject). I may have picked up your vibes before I dreamed for you. Do you have a sore throat? Can you imagine the sore throat a dragon would have?

I went back into the same dream and my grandson is determined to stick with the dragon and raise the child. I ask, "Have you seen her moods?" I caution him not to commit until he's seen the worst and sees if he can live with it. Perhaps this and the sore throat are cautions about their endeavor.

The last dream has me waiting around the edges of the life of a famous person. (The guru?) He asks why I hang out with the dishwasher all the time. I answer, "Because he's the only one that talks about things that interest me."

Still in the dream, I am alone once again. The doorbell rings and I'm given a beautiful bouquet of two dozen yellow roses. I cut the stems very, very short and arrange them in a short vase. The arrangement is stunning. The bell rings again and I'm given a wedding invitation.

I tell Carol, "If it were my dream, I can expect a reward for my work, the flowers and the marriage – a meeting of the minds."

She wrote back that her daughter-in-law just received a yellow rose.

Both of us were excited about the dragon. Can you imagine such a good connection? Dream work and dragons could be considered strange bedfellows. The last conversation we had, she said she had to present the dreams to the rest of her group. Maybe they saw something I didn't as that was the last of our communication.

Knowing she joined me
in the belief that we choose
our lives before we come
into this world. I began
to wonder.

Chapter 31

Will I Ever Marry Again?

Penny is another church acquaintance. Her request is one of several reasons I began my studies of Carl Jung and joined the Haden Institutes' Dream Group Leadership Course. Besides wanting to reach more people with my message, I felt there were often things to be interpreted I didn't understand. I was sure there was a message for her as there was definitely a synchronicity. It was a pretty funny one too, at least to this bystander. Penny didn't think it was funny.

Her question was connected to whether she would remarry and have a home again.

At first I had a hard time making a dream connection with her – or maybe she was providing the hard time. First of all, I neglected to ask her what time she would be going to sleep. This seems to make a difference. After my first seemingly fruitless try, I turned on T.V. and watched most of the Eleven PM news before trying again. At Four A.M., things broke loose and I could hardly handle all that came, it came so fast.

I've found, in the past, that the things I experience in bed, before I think I'm asleep are sometimes vital information to the subject. So I told her exactly what I was going through. Before 4 A.M., my first physical problem was a pain in the left wrist. It may or may not have been her problem. It reminded me of the pain one would have after trying to hold on to something or trying to bring something really heavy close.

Then I had a quick vision of a reluctant passenger (maybe on a tall cruise ship). She had told me she had a fear of heights. This may be saying something of that fear. Knowing she joined me in the belief that we choose our lives before we come into this world, I began to wonder. How would you know for sure, when you choose this life that someone would not insist you go to a high place? Could this be her reluctance I was picking up. Perhaps her reluctance says something about not wanting to be alone. Whatever I say is only a guess, I tell her. It was her mind, not mine. She would know any truths.

My first vision (a quick picture) is of little dogs. Man's best friend. They could account for the sore wrist if they were pulling on the far end of a leash.

After this, considering it was almost time to be awake and noting the lack of answers, I changed the question to, "What is Penny's purpose in this life?"

In the first dream, just before 4 A.M., I bring two dogs to the door of one who is to care for them. I ring the bell. Penny opens the door. I come in and am greeted by two other very small dogs. Penny is drying dishes while her mother washes.

In the second dream, I am to leave. The party is over. The place is not mine. I must make sure everything is back to normal. The two speakers, hired for the party, have left. I open the door and see Penny walking a dog. The ground is slightly frozen. It looks like fun and I want to join her even though my shoes are not proper, not sure footing. She comes and helps me over and around mounds of snow.

In the third dream, I am helping her change her belt. She is standing up. The focus is not on the belt or on her body but on the little metal grasper on the belt. I have to wind it around properly. My husband is trying to help so I have to instruct him also. He asks, "Is this normal?" I say, "Oh, yes."

I thought that all I'd seen was a good sign. Doors were opening. Doors may be of opportunity, spiritual understanding, and/or a new person coming through – all or one. Opening a front door is meeting a new experience, waiting for something new in life. This seems closer to her original question but not a definite answer. It could mean she should not focus on a mate but rather to a new life experience. God knows what we need better than we ourselves.

The dogs recur a lot, I noted. I asked if she had a special connection to animals. To me dogs mean loyalty, faithfulness. Then, again, maybe she's already walked a few opportunities, if the dogs were men. I'm looking for a pun or play on words.

The other symbol that struck me was the belt. To my mind belts hold things together. I asked if perhaps she was bound to tight. It was similar to the pain I felt in the beginning. I included some ideas about symbols' meanings from my favorite dream book. However, buckling the belt is making the connection to one of life's necessities (a man?). He comes along to help.

Another significant symbol is the number two. It could signify balance or a need for such in other areas of her life, or two as in two people, man and woman?

My advice to her was to leave her original question in God's hands, concentrate on her dog-walking job (I was only guessing about the job) and keep opening those doors when opportunity comes knocking.

Penny could find no significance to any of this. I brought up the dogs once more and Penny exploded! Those dogs, those damn dogs! Her ex had two of them and they always took precedence before her. They'd go for Sunday drives depending on what the dogs would enjoy! The dogs got to sit in the front seat while she sat in the back! He treated them better than he treated her! How funny that my dreams picked up on that!

The relationship may have been over but something controlling was lingering. It's been a few years since I saw Penny, but I do know she left the church because she became involved with a man who had ties elsewhere. Her outburst still makes me laugh. I kidded her about it for a long time after. Who could have guessed that connection? Not me!

First came the words,
"Heal your body and
God will reward you."

Chapter 32

How Can I Improve My Finances?

Joanie asked me to take this concern to God. Her immediate family consisted of herself, her husband and an adult son. I agreed to ask God but reminded her that God may see her immediate need as something different. I think this is what happened with her dreams.

First came the words, "Heal your body and God will reward you." This may be the area of her life that God felt should come first. Joanie has many physical problems.

I wrote this, turned the light out and a second vision came in the form of a favorite hymn. *Amazing Grace* began playing through my mind and I knew it wouldn't stop until I put the light on again and wrote it down. I wondered, "Does this mean that Joanie may be in line for a miracle through the grace of God?"

I attempted to go to sleep a third time. There was another vision of a dark sky with gold sparkling lights. As I held to that vision I saw two sets of planes flying in formation toward each other. They mesh and pass perfectly. This had to be a good sign. Then another song began, "You are my guiding light." This told me Joanie had a lot of potential.

In the first dream my husband is sitting next to me on the side of the bed. His back is to me and he is thinking. I get a feeling of much comfort. Soon after this night of dreaming Joanie's husband got a better job.

The next vision is of a lady dressed as if she came from the time of the forties. She has a large brimmed hat worn at a tilt on her head. She holds a book to her chest.

Joanie says she has a framed photo of a relative from long ago in a similar pose, dressed like that. There's one synchronicity.

In the next dream, she is in a house with a group of people. A shot is fired. She wants to move but where to? There is trouble where ever they can afford to go. She decides to stay where she is. I see another possibility is brought up, to move to San Francisco. She again decides to stay and fight.

Joanie told me later that this is the nature of her neighborhood.

I asked her if possibly all this talk of moving was a metaphor for the lack of movement she has in her body. She said I was probably right, but she felt lost when it came to any possibility of self-healing.

In the next dream she is considering taking her teenage son (around 14 or 15) and moving. Someone asks, "But what will he do with his time?" She answers, "Well, if we move near a mall, he can hang out there."

Joanie said this was exactly what was going on in her family. Her son wanted to move in with his girlfriend. He is a little naive for his age and when he is with his girlfriend they spend a lot of time at a mall. A second synchronicity.

In the next and last dream, the decision is made. She is to stay. The rest are leaving. She makes a list of the things she wants to keep: a snow coat, an umbrella, and a partial set of beautiful floral print dishes. These she can sell. She'd never give up her dance lessons.

Still in the dream, her father comes to go over the list with her and figure the price she would have to pay for them. She had not known there would be a price to pay. The list is small so maybe the price will be small. The most important thing she wants to keep, her health, has no price. Her health is priceless. It is up to her and this makes her laugh. It's like a joke she has put over on them. The dishes come to her mind. She might like to keep them and add on to them. She decides not to sell them. She laughs, also, about the dance lessons. Others did not understand her wanting them. Right now, her feet will not let her do the lessons. But she is loosing weight and gaining health. The lessons will be a lot of fun. She can dance in her chair.

Her father calculated as she held her breath. He states, "$12.41." Joanie opens the cash drawer and pays him right there. Her life is now hers.

A final song came, "So I can see, return to me, my melody of love."

Joanie asks how to improve her finances. She is told to heal her body first. This small price ($12.41 according to the dream) will set her free for other things. Our conversation after the dreams revealed her lack of faith in self-healing. Hopefully, the dreams will help her move on.

I wrote to Joanie some of the story of my own healing. When I applied myself to healing my body, God opened doors to new sources of income. The price was not high.

"She was surprised
I saw so much
of her life."

Chapter 33

Mopping Floors Is Good

I met Karen on the Internet. She asked what she needed to do to achieve personal peace.

My first vision that night is of a phone ringing. I jump up to get it, but it only rang once. Then again, it may not have rung at all. It could have been a spiritual hearing and I thought, ah, ha, Karen's essence. She is a very harried person who longs for peace.

I had a lot of feeling-type visions that night. It was like my body was a bunch of nerve endings, jumping. It was not pleasant. Part way through the night I took a Tylenol P.M. This may have cost us the remembrance of a dream or two but, as promised, I reported what did come through. I asked her to tell me if anything rang true, any little thing, please to let me know. The truths that come through help convince other people this three-way communication, her, me, and God, is true.

The second vision is a song. It was unknown to me. It sounded like a Broadway show tune and was fast, words slurred, and fast movements. I listened to the words and then they faded. "I'm just a busy bee. I'm just a ---." I become aware of a stomach pain. This could be hers also? Could her life be affecting her health? Is spirit warning us about this also?

The first dream is of a large, paved sidewalk area that has a large square pit. The inner circumference of the pit contains four or five steps that converge down to a stage in the center. People come from all sides filling up the steps to watch Karen. I'm there to watch Karen. She must be one of the people in the center. How will I know which one is she? Later, writing my letter to her I ask, is this what she sometimes wonders about herself? Who am I?

The second dream switches to a baseball game. We're going into time out. It's time to switch sides. Writing this down it seems to me that a change may be coming in her life.

The dream ends and a new vision begins. It is a new tune – slowed down to a waltz. Perhaps the change will be slower paced.

In dream number three she is in charge of making sure a floor in a commercial establishment gets mopped. She watches us do it. It is not done to her satisfaction. She gets up and mops it again herself. This seems to say that she is a take-charge type person rowing her own boat, driving her own car, and mopping her own floor. Or maybe she is too caught up in detail. I left that for her to answer.

In the next dream she is walking, following a group of people who appear dressed, but barely. They have ultra short shorts, tiny straps on the shoulders. They are going in a doorway. Inside I can make out the backs of people sitting in rows. There is a feeling of anticipation.

Then I see her making a map of a floor. She sections it off in flowing, curving lines. This section chocolate, this vanilla, etc., she notes. She seems to be having fun with her work.

Then what better way to end a night of dreaming than by seeing a performance of the last lines of "All that Jazz" done in a very slow tempo?

Karen wrote back that her dream was to purchase a house big enough, in a warm climate (lack of clothes) where she could take in older people. She is a nurse but has been recently diagnosed with M.S. She has a lot of good years yet but fulfilling this dream would make those years easier. She was surprised I saw so much of her life. The measuring of the floor is exactly what she was doing this past weekend. She found a house and was preparing to put in a new kitchen floor, among other things. She was actually laying it out on graph paper to see how much material it would take. Her children, the dream with the people with little clothing on, were going to help her. The rows of people with her in the center would be her new adult care home. She had recently begun taking a course to obtain a license in this type of business.

Chapter 34

A Year 2000 Graduation Message

Pat was a neighbor of mine who was about to graduate. He is a bright young man and eagerly joined me by acting in a play I wrote and produced for our town's library. He was the first to graduate high school in his family for all he knew, so this was even a bigger deal than usual. For a graduation present he asked me for a dream about his future. The dreams and visions that came through would suit any young person and so I offer it here.

Dear Pat,

Ray and I are very proud of you, and this is just the beginning. We come into this world with two things, our bodies and our talents. Nurture them both and find the reason God put you here at this time. Other young people I have dreamed for, showed them at age 25 still laying the foundation for their life. So proceed with patient persistence.

I asked God for some message to give you. The following are the dreams I had for you last night. I give you my interpretation but, since I am not living your life, you will see the true meanings.

The first sensation I was aware of was an itch, an aliveness in the temple area. Then I knew this night would be for you. Your brain, your being is alive with thoughts, wants, and excitement about your future. A song also came that says you can do and be anything you want and at a greater pace than most people.

The first dream took place in a government house. A rival faction was attempting to take over. You were fighting (hand to hand combat) for things to remain the same as they were. You helped defeat the new people. You then sat by a pond, along with others to contemplate the water. What was in front of each of you, under the water, were the graves and tributes to your personal ancestors. (Parents, grandparents?)

My interpretation is to remember as best you can what people before you have lived and died for. Learn from their successes and their mistakes. And know that new is not always right. Think for yourself. Although, at times the going may be rough, take time for contemplation, relaxation and tuning in to God's voice yourself.

Dream #2 had you in a home where you lived with several other people. Just because you were home all day, they expected you to have supper ready for them when they got home. They had the nerve to examine everything you did. Well, (you thought) I could have gotten a recipe off the Internet but that would mean meeting a guy for ingredients a long way off and killing the dog for meat.

My interpretation here is that there are some things best left to others. Not necessarily cooking. The dreams used this as a metaphor. It does point out the difficulty in living with others. Be independent as soon as you can.

Dream #3 had you inspiring a man to do something he could easily do that would be of help to others. In this dream he was to teach children to fish. You pointed out some older men would enjoy learning this also. You made plans for conducting the classes. You had your ideas well thought out. You went looking for him and found him painting a marvelous sign, complete with a true to life painting of the face of a great fisherman I once knew. The sign said you could fish like him. The trouble was that he was painting it on your favorite comforter. You remarked on it but also said you could buy another one. You looked up to see the love of your life looking for you.

My interpretation is that you should not pass up an opportunity to help others develop their skills. You will help bring pleasure to others and this is a worthy goal. Knowing you and your talents, though, this will more likely be through your acting and not the fishing.

The last part is saying that your mate in life will find you when the time is right. Get on with the more important things like career and helping others. When the time is right, God will bring her into your life. She may already be there, in your life, but first things first. She will wait. You will be a more complete person, have more to offer her and yourself then.

Best of luck, Vi."

Chapter 35

Alzheimer's

Patricia's mother had been living with her for a few years, ever since she was diagnosed with Alzheimer's. Patricia's question concerned their future together. So far the mother has been very calm, childlike and obedient, a pleasure to care for, but care it is. The date of the request is interesting to me and may account for the theme of the dreams. It was June 6, just between Memorial Day, May 31 and July 4, Independence Day.

In my first vision, I often refer to this as an essence, it's as if I'm looking down of a sea of twinkling lights. I see a girl dragging a doll behind her, walking slowly across the lights. I took this to be the mother. It could also be Patricia feeling an endless expanse or experience.

Dream number one has me with a group of people acting out a play for Independence Day. We are in a church, on the stage. Our audience is unknown. We fall into our roles quite naturally. I seem to be setting things up but we are all equally important. I have the American Flag, a huge one we will drape across all of us.

The people in the middle have the speaking parts. All speeches lead up to a need for independence for our nation. The minister (or he could be a congressman) has a meeting to go to afterward where there will be lunch. He asks us if we brought food for ourselves in a tone of voice that suggests we will, of course, take care of ourselves.

The play goes well, no mistakes, very polished like we have done it many times before. As we line up across the front in chairs, my view switches to seeing the actors from the rear. They are all sitting except for the third from the right. He is a huge, friendly, people-like, baboon who squats, dressed in people's clothes. I can see his tail. He watches carefully and follows the rest.

The words were something to the effect, "Today is the day we declare our freedom!" At the end of the play, we're not quite sure what we are to do next.

In the scenario Patricia presented to me, this seemed to restate her problem. What do we do next? I also see a plea for freedom. Probably the family longed for freedom but it crossed my mind that her mother also longed for freedom. The synchronicity of the night was in the fact that just days before the dream, unknown to me, while watching animal planet together they saw a program where a baboon was featured. Patricia's mother became very excited and claimed that animal was herself. She kept pointing at the screen saying me! Me!

The next dream has us strolling through a fair, going from booth to booth. The little boy with us wants everything. I say he has to pick just one. We have a lot of trouble picking one and end up with an inexpensive whistle for him and some more of the same for the children back home.

Patricia explains this dream as the way they live. Everyday of the week Patricia or a friend takes the mother to a mall for diversion, often buying her cheap trinkets.

In the last dream I am doing math problems in my head, long math problems ending with short numbers. I suggest she use math and mind quizzes with mother also.

Chapter 36

Predictions

Sometimes I get dreams that seem to be for society at large. One such came to me in early May of 2004. As you know, I gave up beef in 1985. This dream seemed to be telling me to give up chicken and I wondered what I was going to eat. I stuck with the chicken but after a few months, T.V. ads began warning us of tampered chicken. This was long before all the talk of bird flu.

In the dream I am with a team of food inspectors. Chicken is being sold black market, below average market prices, from hidden camps of poachers who raise less than perfect birds. They cook and package them and mark them with children's stickers. We talk to workers in a distribution plant where we find some of these packages. They finally see our point, that we need to find the source and they mention seeing smoke from chicken fires off in the hills across the lake.

We follow their directions, see the smoke ourselves and sneak near to a camp before we meet our first poacher. Questions are raised about activities further up the hill. I become aware we are about to bag either a big politician or a rich person.

As I said, I didn't like this dream and it's implications for me. Chicken is my meat of choice. When ads for chicken started telling us to use this brand, because it was pure and not tampered with, I knew to take this message seriously. Perhaps it is a warning. Perhaps it is a glimpse into the future.

Another message seems to be trying to smooth out relationships in general. It told me great floods are coming. The world would be covered with water. If we are busy with hatred for someone, we will be left adrift on a piece of floating flooring with that person or people until the time we come to have empathy for that person. If we continue to hate, we will continue to drift together.

Those of us who carry only love in our hearts will be adrift on party boats with lots of good food and no worries. We'll enjoy the adventure and soon find a spot of beauty to land on and start anew.

I experienced another dream the same night. I was told that the beginning of the change would be signaled by a growing number of people with addictions. People with addictions to anything will be naked to everyone's view. I see a female lying helplessly naked in front of a crowd of people. She is the symbol of all addictions for pills lie all around her. One of her old friends comes along and covers her up, gets help and chases away the crowd. One person who cares makes a huge difference.

Yet we know we really can't be helped until we want change. The words came, "Before you reach that point of lying naked before the crowd, be the one to help save yourself. Make that needed change in yourself. Be your own best friend."

Chapter 37

Essence

I hear you asking, what is this thing I call 'essence'?

You might think of the essence of an apple as its odor or the way it feels in your fingers, it's taste in your mouth, and its crunch, or lack of, when you bite into it. It's like nothing else. Closing your eyes, picture a spiritual apple, complete and beautiful before it's born. See the flower on an apple tree. It has unseen potential to grow to fill that image. It's happened so many times, we expect this to happen. The essence of the apple waits, unseen, to become a whole apple.

We, also, have unseen potential. However, the choices we make in life often spoil the perfect, beautiful self we were meant to be. Unlike the apple, a person's essence changes with each choice we make along our path. Your present essence can be captured in dreams as the pain you are experiencing or the promise in life you're either fulfilling or not fulfilling. When this missing link to your spiritual you comes through, it speaks volumes about you as a person.

Depending on who is dreaming about whom, the essence can change. If I dream about someone difficult in my life, I'll get one essence. I'll get what they mean to me for the purpose of dealing with our relationship. How a person is difficult to me and how they are to someone else might be different. Then that person's own dream essence will be different. If they ask me to dream for them, I see things from their soul's point of view, something essential to their happiness. That's four different essences.

Essence is not potential, like the growth of the apple, it is who we are at that moment in time through the eyes of each of the four different people. To me, this difficult person may be a brick wall, to himself, a mountain climber. A third party who asks for a message about this difficult person may receive a pain. Or maybe to that third person this person is not difficult but lovable. She might see a teddy bear. If I'm asked by him to dream for him I might see his true potential, something that would take him out of the difficult and into a more satisfying way of life, perhaps a leadership ability or a talent.

As I dream for another person, at their request, I'm in their mind, sometimes seeing what should be. I've been shown a person's talent that they've secretly wanted to spend time with, and the angels agree. This is good for them. They're being prodded to spend more time with this. It will open doors of opportunity for them as it did for me.

Your essence will change as you mature.

The essence is the first thing I receive, sometimes even before I go to sleep. Just as my head hits the pillow I'll have a vision. One lady's initial vision came as a computer spewing out page after page of writing. When questioned, she said she was a "closet poet"! She shared some of her poems with me and they were very inspirational, based on lessons learned raising a Down's Syndrome child. After our dream, she submitted a poem to her church's national magazine. It was accepted and she became a regular contributor to that publication.

The first vision for Mary, (Chapter 17) was of sexual feelings, for instance. It let me know I was in her subconscious and probably seemed out of context with the pattern of the rest of the dreams that night. The other dreams were all about Mary's need to sell her vacation property and her next career, and answered her questions about the things she should be doing with her life, right now.

That mini-dream, or vision, has everything to do with who Mary is, as a person, at that particular point in time. It's part of her essence.

Other examples are the hammering I heard the night I dreamed for the carpenter (in chapter 1). Gail's essence (chapter 5) came through in the first dream about being in a dry, useless desert. Another person, who raises horses, brought me the odor of horses and hay.

Our essence is a highly important, yet often elusive key to happiness. The dictionary defines essence as the quality or qualities that create identity. This basic information about a dream subject often comes through just as I lay my head on my pillow, even before I'm really asleep.

One type of essence is talent. A lady came through as a ballerina, something she'd pursued throughout her childhood. As a result, she went back to dance class and made it a part of her life again. Several people I've dreamed for have used the information about their essence to bring balance into their lives. If it has something to do with our intended path, opportunities will open up.

For some reason most of us tend to stifle our talents. For instance, one person I know well has a wonderful talent for drawing. She feels it's nothing compared to the talents of others and, therefore, does not pursue art. Perhaps her life would become less stressful if she set aside a few minutes each day to draw. Who knows where the practice and the experience might lead. A great opportunity might open for her.

We come into this world with few things. Our talents are among them. They help us fill the role we came to play.

The very first mini-vision I receive while dreaming for others doesn't seem to come in dreams for myself. Your own essence is shown in your own dreams as an ongoing theme. When there is a major shift in your way of seeing yourself, your essence and your dream scene will change.

Essence reflects not only your talents but also those things currently taking center stage in your life. My essence, at first, was that of a struggling mother. Then I saw my male side waking up as I became better able to manage my life.

Your essence can also be pain. The story of Frank (chapter 2) started with a sharp pain in each foot. Think on the old saying of shooting yourself in the foot. This also applies to this vision. He was not doing all he could to help himself.

Dreams are also good personality barometers. Look to see if you are solving others' problems or serving others. Maybe you are running away from something. You can't always change these things, but the dream action will change suddenly one day, letting you know you've taken a step forward.

Part Three

The Mechanics
Of
Dreaming For Others

"In working with your own dreams, a note left under your pillow, a note containing your question for God that you have first held and prayed over, will bring the same results."

Chapter 38

―――――⊶⟊⊷―――――

The Mechanics of Dreams For Others Vs. One's Own

"Vi, is the process of dreaming for others any different from that of dreaming for myself?" I ask.

"The results are different," Vi replies, "A person asks for a dream and I have them write their name, address and phone number on a piece of paper with their question. This way, if events between the asking and my going to sleep are hectic, this piece of paper brings their essence back to me as I hold it and pray for guidance for them. A night of answers begins."

Vi continues, "In working with your own dreams, a note left under your pillow, a note containing your question for God that you have first held and prayed over, will bring the same results."

I remember asking, "Is this where you get this peek into their essence?"

"Yes," Vi says. "After the essence, I receive a re-stating of the question. Sometime during the night comes the synchronicity. The stories will include something about the person, some small thing in their life I would have no way of knowing such as left-handedness, the nationality of their ancestors; enlightening things like a collection of something they own. This is validation for the person that I was in communication with their soul. Closer to morning, there will be a story to alter their thinking. It will help them return to their path. They always understand this better than I do."

"Do they need to have a specific question, or is just 'dream for me' okay?" I ask.

Vi answers, "Either way. If they have a specific question, they should be as clear to me as possible. They'll get a more satisfactory answer. Even different wording can bring different answers. It's like the difference between asking may I or can I. It helps to make sure, to the best of your knowledge, that this is the most important question in your life, right now. God will answer any concern, but I've found that His view of what is important for you right now, and yours, may be two different things. He will prod you to the path you need to be on."

"A lot of my dreams for myself are just a reliving of what I did the day before," I said.

Vi nodded yes and added, "This seems true of both dreaming for others and my own dreams. I've found that what I think are simply a replay of exactly what I do each day: go to the office, clean the house, take care of the children, etc., is actually the other way around. Everything in life is lived first in the dream state. This explains deja vu.

"Don't forget," cautions Vi, "Dreams are exaggerations. Don't expect answers to be exact. Look instead for some smaller good to come into your life, if you dream of winning the lottery. Look for a monetary gift, a better job, a payment of something someone owed you, a compliment."

Vi continued, "Dreams are exaggerations because God is trying to bring a feeling to you rather than an actual happening. That's because we have to make our own choices. Our strong gut feelings give us a strong will, which helps when making decisions, or breaking an addiction. You'll feel lucky to get the job, the raise, etc., somewhat like the luck you feel in a dream involved with winning the lottery.

"Knowing the dream action might be predictive gives you clues. It may happen today or a couple of weeks from now. You can use the dream information to make better decisions. You'll put off making some decisions because a dream has shown you a different ending."

I ask, "So, if you dream for me today and again in a year, the dreams will be different?"

"The advice changes from day to day," Vi replied.

"Could those exaggerations seem like nightmares?" I wondered

"Oh, yes," Vi said, "Some dream stories are exaggerations meant to scare us, show us the outcome of our actions should we continue down our present path. It can spur us on to faster, more positive, waking actions.

"Often the dream you get just before waking, however, seems

too good to be true, like wishful thinking. It is showing the feeling we can have if we change our path or our way of thinking on some part of our life. The last dream in my dreams for others usually still discusses the problem. Life hands out the solution based on your choices."

"Are the stories that take place over a week or a month all about the same thing?" I asked.

"Often," Vi answered. "It helps to have remembered the earlier ones. That's why it's good to keep a dream journal. Some time, when you write the dream, one word or phrase might jump out at you; struggle, did before, lonely, being led, could not keep my head on straight. You will realize this is the whole message as you relate it to something going on in your life.

"Or," she said, "Your dream may be a report card on something you did yesterday. Our angels often rate our performance during the day just past. This accounts for any obvious rehashing. Sometimes I look at the "I" figure as being my guardian angel. If "I'm" frustrated, think how frustrated my guardian angel must be trying to get me on the right path."

I laughed at the thought of a frustrated angel. I said, "You make it sound as though there is a divine plan for each of us."

Vi answered, "Our soul comes into this world with a goal. It has ideals and if we don't live up to them, if our angels don't like our method of dealing with a particular situation, they will let us know. Bottom line is, there is someone, unseen, smarter than us, who knows all there is to know about us and cares about what's good for us. This spirit loves us and tries to help us. We have a big brother, a mother, a father, a mentor, and a higher self in our dreams."

Vi continued, "If you wake exhausted and/or unhappy, you may have been warring with your higher self over some action you took the day before. When you wake happy it's because your higher self is content with the way you're living your life."

"I'm going to be afraid to miss a dream," I said.

"Don't worry," Vi replied, "When you miss recalling a dream, you still have clues to working with spirit. A tired and unhappy feeling can prompt you to review your actions from the day before. You'll find an error, a situation you might have handled differently, or not at all. Try to avoid this kind of situation in the future, and show your higher spirit that you are trying to make your life better based on what you perceive He is telling you. It will help. The message will return until you do get the message."

"Does being sick have any bearing on my dreams?" I ask.

"Yes," Vi says, "If you have pain in your legs, your dream will include that feeling by having you running. A story is needed to surround this feeling and probably will show you being chased. The truth of the dream is a message to take better care of yourself so your legs won't throb. If your stomach's overfull or gassy, you might see a scene of drowning or of being taken over by something. It's actually true. If you had not had that particular food, you'd be free for more important messages. This is a temporary condition, but most important to be addressed at this point in time. Food and stress can be controlled. When you get beyond these problems, the bigger picture of your life comes into focus.

"By the same token," Vi continued. "When you are bothered by disease-like symptoms, you can ask God why? Write it on a piece of paper to pray over and leave under your pillow as you go to sleep. Chances are that you will get directions to repair your body."

I liked that. "So," I said, "I will be able to make better choices. That would be nice."

"With dreams, we are given a chance to avoid mistakes entirely," Vi said. "You sometimes get a story showing a point of view you'd not thought of before. In my case, the point of view was never mine or the other persons, it was from a perspective neither of us had in mind. It's like we all, sometimes, get caught up in being right and we don't even understand the question. Or we take life at surface value when it really is very deeply involved."

"Some people will think I'm crazy if I mention my dream!" I blurted out.

Smiling, Vi replied, "When you're working toward a personal healing, belief in what you are doing is most important. Therefore, it is better not to tell anyone what and why you are doing anything until you see results. You don't need anyone to put doubts in your mind. You must keep a positive attitude. Sharing your method of healing with others, no matter how needy they might be, opens you to their negativity and ridicule. If you want good results, you must not be swayed by doubt."

I ask, "Would it help to own a dream dictionary?"

She says, "Buy a couple of dream dictionaries. Use them to open doors to the meanings of words and actions in your dreams. One symbol can mean different things to different people based on each ones' life experiences and daily living. That's why I leave the final interpretation of the dreams to the person I dream for."

My turn. "You said before that everything in the dream is you. Explain please."

She obliges saying, "Look at every person, every thing in your dream as a different aspect of yourself, of your personality. If you dream of a co-worker who pushes everyone aside to get a promotion, look to an area of your life where you may be pushing someone aside. Then think on the opposite side. Are you letting go too easy?

"Objects are you, also. If an object like a suitcase, for example, appears in the dream it signifies something going on in your life also. Are you being ignored, shut away in a closet? Stuffed full? Are you allowing yourself to be used by someone? Are you feeling kicked around? It might suggest unopened situations that you must face.

Vi continued. "As you go along you'll create your own dream dictionary. Do it in the back pages of your dream journal. Title your dreams and save the first page of your journal as a table of contents. It is easier to look back and find dream predictions after they actually happen. Something will click, I dreamed that! This makes dream recall exciting."

"Do dreams, over a period of time relate to each other?" I asked.

"Yes," Vi says, "When reviewing your dreams, remember that each one builds on the last. You are being shown the same situation by way of a different story until you finally get the message. Look for a common theme or action."

"That's a lot to think about," I say and then laugh and ask, "Can I overcome my natural tendency to be stubborn, do things my own way no matter what the dreams seem to be saying?"

"Deep question," Vi says, "It's not always up to us. Attitude changes take place even without your knowledge or work. When your dreams show you going to the bathroom, often in a very public place, this is a sign of letting go of a way of thinking and a change. You can become a calmer person, patient, smile more, be able to let things that used to get under your skin now roll off your back."

Vi added, "Your dreams come from four primary sources. The first is your own subconscious. Here you will review yesterday's actions, things you've repressed, or receive health warnings before anything is physically obvious. You can make changes. The dream will let you know how to relate to people, to your career, or perhaps tell you how to handle your investments. It will warn you of possible problems with your car or other things you face in day-to-day encounters.

"A second source is the subconscious mind of another person. It's a way of communicating with someone around the block or across the country. Some would call it mental telepathy. It also explains my dreaming for others. I intercept what God is trying to tell them because they haven't yet developed their own ability to receive or understand.

"A third primary source is the super conscious, the universal, etheric stream of intelligence or God's record book. Everything known and waiting to be known is floating in the ether around us. If you are a scientist, spending much time on one particular subject, information on this subject will become available to you.

"Often I have come up with a great idea for an invention only to see that same thing announced in the paper as being invented by someone else. Writers and artists receive inspiration here, sometimes two or three receive the same thing, at the same time.

"Predictions of community and world events come through here. I need not act on them. They are a marking of God's time. They convince me of the reality of the etheric stream of intelligence.

"And the fourth source is God, Himself. I have received essays on world affairs and solutions. Things I never would have believed have become clear to me. One thing that brought me a laugh was a vision of the Hasbalad and the Israelis' playing football with each other. It made me wonder if this was God's wish for that area.

"Predictions on a personal level let me make changes to avoid certain happenings or, if not avoidable, cushion myself for life's shocks. Shocks bring stress. I have a delicate constitution (as my Grandmother would call it). Stressful events or negative people make me ill. God does not want me sick. So He warns me of upcoming days that could be trying. These dreams are quite clear."

I had one last question, "What happened to the marina?"

"We sold it in 1992," Vi said, "The pressure remained all that time and we couldn't wait to get out. If it wasn't the neighbors fighting us, it was the pressures of running a business, dealing with less than ethical bankers and attorneys, it was getting up in the middle of the night to retie boats that were being blown around by the wind. Maybe we should have chosen Florida back then. I have come to believe things happen for a reason.

"The new owners are part of a corporation and are much more politically savvy than we were. They continue to reconstruct the property. They've been able to get a series of grants to provide public access to the lake.

"One of the first things they did was to bring public water to the marina and it's neighbors. One thing has not changed for them. The new owners are continually fending off attacks by the neighbors, even when there's nothing to fight about. When I hear those stories, I think, better them than us.

"We stay in touch. We love the property and regret letting it get away, but I'm convinced I will live long enough to see something just as great in my life and just as pleasurable come from my dream work. That is God's gift to me and it's really grown since moving away from the life I had in New York State."

"This gives new meaning to the old phrase 'stress is a killer,'" I say.

"In more ways than one," Vi confirms.

Recommended Reading:

Children's Past Lives: How Past Life Memories Affect Your Child by Carol Bowman
Our Dreaming Mind by Robert Van de Castle
Many Mansions by Gina Cerminara
Women Who Run With The Wolves by Clarissa Pnkola Estes
Dream Language by Robert Hoss
Balancing Heaven and Earth by Robert A. Johnson
Inner Work by Robert A. Johnson
Dreams, Memories, Reflections by C.G. Jung
Life After Life by Raymond A. Moody, Jr. M.D.
Reflections on Life After Life by Raymond Moody, Jr. M.D.
Dream Medicine by Henry Reed
The Man Who Wrestled With God by John Sanford
Where People Fly and Water Runs Uphill by Jeremy Taylor
Discovering Your Soul's Purpose by Mark Thurston, Ph.D.
Explore Your Past Lives by Mark Thurston, PhD

Dream Symbols Dictionary
The meanings if it were my dream ..

Accident: A warning, see vehicles. Be careful in the next few days. Better yet, what decisions have you made that may be leading you in the wrong direction? Don't be hasty with new decisions in the next week or two. If something broke, either it wasn't meant to be or the timing wasn't right.

Acquaintance: Share the dream with this person as it may be a message for him\her rather than yourself. Examine how you think about the person. Is he\she a cheat, is he\she strong and controlling, is he\she making a mistake? Apply these attributes to yourself or someone taking a new role in your life right now. Is this new venture or person possibly going to end up like the person in your dream?

Age: If you see yourself as an old person, look to your overall health or listen to the words of wisdom this ancient one speaks. Look at the age of the dream characters. If they are younger than you, they may represent a youthful attitude you may have about something in your waking life. Act your age! Could be the age of a project now in your life, and the dream may be referring to it. Think back to what happened to you at that age. It may be still controlling your life.

Apron: Wearing one is a cover-up, are you fooling yourself about something? Is someone else fooling you? Protection. Maybe company is coming that you need to prepare for.

Attic: Your spiritual level of consciousness. If it is an old attic, most likely you are receiving help from loved ones now in spirit. It's also a place to find treasures.

Baby: New life, new direction or opportunity. You may be giving birth to your higher self. Need for more understanding, compassion. Look to something in your life for which you do not have a mature attitude. Put yourself in the place of the baby in your dreams. Are you allowing yourself to be treated like a baby? How is that baby being treated?

Backwards: If you are traveling backwards in your dreams, you are also doing that in life. Once I dreamed I was in a car driven by my son, his girlfriend was in the front seat with him. We were traveling backwards until we went over a cliff. It referred to my son's relationship with that girlfriend. The relationship soon ended.

Bait: See fishing.

Balcony: Higher than others, this indicates you are moving ahead on your spiritual path. Observe.

Ball: Learn to play the game (perhaps the game of life.) Notice the action of the ball. I once dreamed of a ball bouncing on a sidewalk. It split in two. One half fell dead, the other bounced higher, freer. I thought this was a description of the recent marital breakup of a woman for whom I was dreaming. Perhaps it was saying to get on with her life. She said, "No, I used to be a clown and a ball was part of my act." She saw it as part of her essence.

Basement: Your obsessions, closer to your subconscious. Find old issues that hold you hostage.

Bathroom, going to the bathroom: Eliminating or needing to eliminate a negative attitude from your life. See eliminations

Bees: Very busy. Are you being industrious or stressful?

Bible: Religious thoughts. Try to find the part mentioned. Is the book old, falling apart? You need to examine your beliefs.

Bike: An interesting sidelight in your life. See vehicles.

Binoculars: A need to see things more clearly.

Birds: Heavenly messengers or a part of you that needs to be set free.

Bleeding: Occurred often in my dreams until things straightened out in my life. I think it symbolized a letting go of something I held close, something I wouldn't believe was wrong for me if you told me regarding jealousy, hatred, obstructing myself.

Boat: Your temporary vehicle of life. Perhaps you have angelic help to get over the rough waters of life. Have faith you are not alone in your troubles.

Books: Take these as messages from The Great Book of Learning, your soul's record. Contact with your recording angel.

Borrow: Look elsewhere for a proper attitude. Not being true to yourself about something. You can't own it!

Bouquet: A reward. Or, perhaps, take a look at the kind of flowers contained in the bouquet. Daffodil = joy; Daisy = goodwill message between mankind; Dandelion = strength, healing, rebirth. See lilac.

Bowling: A message about how you are playing the game of life. Something is about to be won, given up or the rules changed. (Once, for myself, I dreamed of aiming a bowling ball and throwing it down the alley. The alley began to heave like the waves of an ocean. The ball came back to hit me, knocking me down. Two days later I had a car accident ending my plans for that week. God needed me elsewhere.)

Box: Be careful of getting yourself in a difficult position. Is it empty? You have the chance to fill it with the things you want.

Bride: May be indicative of a meeting of the minds with someone. A reward or pat on the back for good works.

Bridge: Crossing over into another land in your dreams, or taking an important spiritual step in waking life. Crossing over chaos (grace).

Bugs: Impending colds or flu. What's bugging you?

Building (under construction): Something not yet resolved. Something building.

Burglar: Someone is about to cheat you. You may be missing an important point. Go back to sleep and give him what he wants, knowing God supplies your true needs. Put yourself in the place of the burglar, what do you want from life that you're not getting.

Burning: A cleansing.

Bus: The life trip you are taking that involves neighbors or the community at large, how you fit in. Some of mine have been so bizarre that I adopted the viewpoint of another researcher. (She felt she was being used to visit mental hospitals in the night for the purpose of spiritual healing.) I began to pray for all sick people after that. See vehicles

Cage: You are not comfortable in your current position. If a bird resides there, let him loose.

Camera: You will soon be getting the picture, gain understanding about what is really going on. God knows you are trying. (Once I dreamed a photographer was to take my picture. He told me to go home and drink more milk. My color would be better then.) It was a health warning.

Candy: A reward or an indulgence. A possible need for discipline.

Cannibals: Someone is being selfish.

Car: Your personal vehicle through this life. Look at the kind of car. For years, mine was a Volkswagon Beetle. I did own one for a short time long ago. I believe this spoke of humbleness, how I thought of myself, or humbleness of my financial picture. Are you driving a Mercedes? What would that say about you? Perhaps you're being driven. The ideal position would be behind the steering wheel, totally in control. It might be good to be outside your car, polishing it up if you've been feeling weak. Perhaps you have a flat tire or motor problems. Something in your life needs fixing or can be fixed. See vehicles

Card game: Are you playing by the rules? If you are the cards, is someone dealing you fairly?

Cash register: Now might be a good time to review your budget or your food intake. I took a dream of paying for lunch with lettuce leaves to mean that I should add more lettuce to my diet. The cash register may be a reminder about your actions being registered in the Book of Life. Do you want whatever you are doing, feeling or thinking to be on your record?

Casket: When I have seen this, it has meant a death.

Cathedral or church: Entering a holy place while asleep.

Chains: May indicate your growth, building, adding links. Is it finished yet?

Chair: If you are sitting in it, you are not using your will power. You may need to relax about something. Find your place.

Chalk: The writing on a chalkboard is a direct message, as "the writing is on the wall".

Cheering or applause: Good job!

Children: The maturity of your current attitude about something. Are you acting like a five year old? The maturity of your shadow (something you've repressed, good or bad) as it comes out of your unconscious.

Circus: In life we go from stage to stage; in a circus the performers go from ring to ring. Put more fun in your life. What are the performers doing?

City Hall: Someone in authority is sending you a message. To judge or not.

Cliffs: Climbing = you are doing well. Falling over = not so well.

Clothes: Color is important. Or, they may tell you about a past life.

Clown: You are being fooled or not facing reality. Are you hiding behind a mask?

Coffin: Someone has died.

College: We continue to learn, sometimes during the day, sometimes at night. Relax and let it happen. You may be feeling insecure about something in your life, similar to when you were in school. Searching for answers.

Colors: See how you feel about a color. Black is not always depressing. To me it often comes as an indication of the unconscious. White is purity and God's heavenly light of love; pink is love; blue might be spirituality, peace, or feeling blue; green means healing.

Community: The setting of your life. A commercial setting will refer to your work life. A bedroom community may mean something else.

Construction: God isn't finished with you yet.

Cop: An authority figure. Are you getting instructions, a pat on the back, help, or a reprimand?

Corner: Time to turn a corner in your life, perhaps. Use your best judgment.

Costume: Could be a scene from a past life.

Crossroads: You are at a crossroads in your life. Which way will you turn? Is there a new opportunity? Who's driving your car?

Crustacean: I once dreamed a small snail-like creature scurrying down the sidewalk before me but standing upright on two legs. She was coughing badly. I immediately identified the creature as a woman I knew, a crusty little person. She did come down with a bad cold soon after.

Crown: A great reward is being bestowed for spiritual growth.

Cup of tea: Beware gossip. Take a break. Reminiscent of the Boston Tea Party perhaps there's something that should be thrown out.

Cup of water: Beginnings of a purification. Or more water is needed in your body.

Daises: A flower of love or frustration.   Is someone pulling your petals unnecessarily, annoying you? Don't let them.

Dance: Observe rhythms, like slow down, speed up, etc. Apply to your life.

Dawn: A new opportunity, see things in a new light.

Death: Expect a change. It could be as subtle as a change of attitude on your part or the biggest thing you can imagine. Maybe they are both the same. Learning to pore your milk is a death to the one who couldn't pore his milk.

Desert: Hot and dry like your life?

Dessert: Something sweet is coming into your life or you are being given a pat on the head. You are doing good and deserve a reward. Maybe you need to eliminate this from your diet!

Door: Opportunities. Is it open or closed. If closed, maybe you are not to pursue something. Close the door on that idea.

Driving: You are in charge of your life. This is good. Look where you are going.

Ducks: Consider what you feel about the animal you see. Watch their actions. They may be trying to tell you something. I recently saw them sitting on the ground, in a file, barely alive. They needed to be set free. I needed to get out of the house and breathe some fresh air.

Earth: Freshly plowed means to extricate yourself from a dirty situation, be it a matter of health, in your mind, or in your morals. Go back to basics.

Earthquake: Watch the news to see if this was a prediction. If not, a shake up is needed in some area of your life. May be a warning that your life is about to be turned upside down.

Echo: Repeat.

Eggs: New life.

Eliminations: Whenever I see myself in the bathroom, I know I am ready to drop a wrong attitude. If people are watching me in the dream, it means a very public attitude. It doesn't matter because I'm ready to change my mind and often don't even realize I have changed my feelings on a subject. I'm fine tuning me.

Exercise: Do it.

Face: How did the face make you feel? Do we need to "get in your face"?

Falling: At night we leave our bodies. The falling you feel when awaking is a sudden return to your body. No problem. Or, you may be headed for a disappointment. See where you can change something.

Farm: Back to basics, good nutrition, new beginnings or harvest.

Feet: Your foundation. The shoes give a clue to this life or another.

Fence: Either you see beyond the fence or you do not. The state of your spiritual outlook or willingness to see others' point of view. A white fence is heavenly protection; brick is a materialistic protection; old is abuse. See wall.

Fire: A cleansing. If fire is controlled you are protected. If out of control, beware of hatred. Could signal a fever.

Fire engine: Perhaps this has something to do with your passions. Is something consuming you? A fire engine may be there to save you.

Fishing: You are meeting the great Fisherman, Jesus. If you are an avid fisherman, it could be a way of showing you something about your life. Spending too much time (or not enough) on repeating actions.

Flood: Could be a prediction. Could be a warning not to get carried away with something or let yourself be caught up in anything you can't handle.

Flying: A very spiritual thing to do. The first time I achieved this I was energized for a week or more. It is great. Say to yourself on going to bed, "I will fly tonight." It's a step in controlling your dreams, to create what you want. You may only get it if it is okay with God's plan or it may bring a lesson, so watch what you wish for.

Fog: You are not seeing something clearly.

Food: A health warning. Change your diet.

Fork in the road: Either you just made an important decision or a decision is coming up.

Forgery: Beware of deceit, your own or others. Your inner self knows and does not let you get away with it.

Foundation: Your foundation, what makes you who you are. Have you built it well? One person's foundation was described as strong chain links forming a square, with the sides being love, peace, work, and play. I have also seen it as a Parcheesi board, a game we move around. I was one of the pieces. If one side is longer than the others, adjust your life. A perfect square was needed. Balance these areas of your life.

Frightened: There is something you must pay attention to - now! You may be punishing yourself.

Fruit: Add it to your diet.

Fun: Is it missing from your life? Do something about it.

Funeral: A death, or learning the meaning of death to aid your soul growth.

Gambling: You are taking unnecessary chances in life.

Game: It is not whether you win or lose but what game you are playing and how you are doing it. Would God approve?

Garden: Take time to relax, smell the roses. Nurture something. Time for harvest.

Gasoline: Your physical energy may be low or your car may be in need of gas.

Gems: Good fortune, a gift.

Ghost: Probably bringing you a warning. Spirits are not much smarter than they were in life and sometimes carry forward prejudices. Ask God for your answers to life questions.

Gift: A gift is coming. It may be small, but recognize that you knew ahead of time. You will encourage more.

Girl: Could be the Mother Mary. It could be another side of yourself. What is she doing?

Glass: Note if you are seeing through it or not. If you see beyond the walls, you are thinking intuitively. This is a step forward.

Grapes: Add fruit to diet. If pressing or walking on them, you are squeezing the essence from circumstances. It may be pointing to the fruits of your spiritual vine, earning Grace from God, a coming spiritual blessing.

Green: The color of healing and abundance.

Gun: A statement on your power or a reference to what is powerful in your life, a talent you should be using, asserting your authority, not allowing someone steal your power.

Hair: Is it full and healthy, or thinning, bleak, it may be a health report.

Hall: You are in a passage to another of life's opportunities. Are you caught in a hall and not understanding you have a choice?

Look to the open doors. Go back to sleep asking God to show you what's behind the next door.

Handwriting: I've seen handwriting on a wall or blackboard. The message was very direct, I did not belong where I was because I am psychic. In other words, be who you are.

Harmony as in music: A comment on your state of being.

Heart: Pain in the heart may involve an emotional struggle.

Hedge: See fence or wall. May also be a play on words, as in "hedge your bets", or hedge your answer. You only see partially.

Hole: Don't fall into something. Or it may be a need to dig deeper.

Horse: God's messenger bringing you an easier way to travel. Love him.

House: The place in a house in which the dream story is set relates to the level of your dream. Basement is a very physical, base level such as the foundation of your actions. The first floor is everyday happenings. The kitchen relates to your immediate family. Second floor and up are the higher levels of consciousness. The windows, if you are seeing through them, indicate seeing something from a spiritual perspective. A porch is where you overlook a scene, perhaps in a loved one's life.

Hurricane: Could be the actual prediction of one, somewhere on this planet. It could relate to the way things are happening in your life.

Jail: You are feeling boxed in about your choices. Time to break free for a breather, some fresh air, or a whole change of scenery.

Jewel: A gift is coming your way. Remember, good things come in small packages. Does not always denote a huge gift, just a gift.

Joy: Often comes in dreams to balance out the joy missing in our daytimes. They are called compensating dreams. A prediction or a pat on the back.

Juggler: I would look to the various things in my life. Have I taken on too much? Is there something I can let go? Am I, perhaps, being juggled (pushed) by someone else?

Keel: If you see a sailboat with a deep keel (center board), rough water may be ahead; but you have the strength to keep yourself upright, to see you through. Remember - everything happens for a reason.

Key: You hold the answer to your problem. There is a change you
    must make.

Keyhole: You have a clue to something that will soon take on greater
    importance.

Kill: Unresolved anger lies within. Work on it. What are you doing to
    yourself? Could you be your own worst enemy?

Kitten: Any time you see an animal, consider how you feel about that
    animal. Do you view kittens as cute playthings or sneaky
    individuals? This may be a commentary on someone in your
    life, or your subconscious may be editing some of your own
    thoughts. Give yourself some cuddling.

Knife: Anything may be literal, but symbolically this may mean you
    are on the cutting edge of great things. It could be a play on
    words for "get the point?" Could be punctuation. If a group of
    people wave knives and then suddenly sheath them, a change is
    coming, a bad time is over.

Ladder: You are making headway in your endeavors. You are being
    shown an opportunity to step up your spiritual side, or are you
    being congratulated for your spiritual growth.

Laugh: Good times are either ahead or you need to put more laughter
    in your life. A prediction of disturbing news that you are not to
    take too seriously. Is Spirit laughing at you or with you?

Laundry: Something you have held secret may be about to come out.
    Your dreams would not bring it up if you were not ready to
    face it.

Law: A higher authority, a message from an angel.

Lazy: A lack of energy that might happen because of the pace you are
    presently keeping. A warning to slow down. May also be a
    commentary on your own growth, materially and spiritually.
    The day you, or the character in your dream that is always
    sleeping wakes up, that will mark a significant move forward.
    Not motivated.

Learn: The tough things in life are there to teach us spiritual lessons.
    When learning in our dreams, it is paralleled to our waking life.

Leaves: Can denote a time of year or be a message that things fall, we
    rest, and life returns. Biding your time waiting for God's
    timing.

Ledger: Things must balance. To let one thing take over a large part of your life is a sin against your self. Balance family, work, recreation, and spirit. Or you may actually need to sit down with all involved and work on the family plan. Keeping track of your spiritual progress.

Lemon: Old sayings mean a lot to my way of interpretation. If I were to have lemons in my dream, I would recall the saying, "When handed lemons, make lemonade." Then again, you may need lemons in your diet.

Lesson: See learn.

Letter: Try to recall the writing, the message.

Light: God shining on you. The end of a problem is in sight such as "the light at the end of a tunnel." It does not have to be a tunnel, simply the light. You suddenly will see things from a different perspective, which will change everything. New evidence. A healing.

Lilacs: Do they remind you of a loved one's perfume? She is visiting you. I would consider lilacs as a spiritual gift as they have always been my favorite flower. They'd be like getting an A on my life's report card.

Lion: What comes to your mind when you think of this animal? Due to a meditation, I have taken a lion (or tiger) as my healing helper. When in pain, I visualize him inside me, eating the problem and spitting it out. This, I have come to believe, activates and guides my immune system thru that particular problem. It works for me. Could be aggression.

Lizard: I would take this as pointing to someone in my life. See crustacean.

Lock: Turn away, give up some action. It is not for you at this time. Spirit will tell you when the time is right. Guard something.

Lord: Any authority figure in your dream would be a messenger of the Lord. He would never tell you to do anything wrong. If you are being shown wrong doing, it is because these thoughts are in your heart and you need to analyze them. Wrong doing may be a symbol of some wrong you are committing against yourself.

Lottery: I once asked God to give me the winning lottery numbers. A "voice" came load and clear, "You have to learn how to earn your money."

Luggage: This may be a symbol of yourself. How is it being treated? What can you do differently? Do you feel overstuffed, neglected, in a closet?

Lunatic: Sometimes we travel to hospitals in our dreams to give learning or support to people who are ready to die but have not yet crossed. Maybe you or someone close is way off base about something. Get a grip!

Lungs: A health warning. God gave us the breath of life. If we don't protect what He gave us, how can we expect Him to give us more? Also, we are reminded that judging is suffocating us. Is a situation smothering you?

Machinery: Find out more about the workings of a situation.

Maid: Are you taking care of everyone in your dreams? This may be the stage of life you are progressing through. Life comes in stages, unless we refuse to grow.

Mail: Something important is coming in the mail, or don't miss this message from God.

Man: If an unknown man appears, see how you feel about him; notice his essence. Is he someone to learn from? To fear? Do you envy what he does for a living? Take it up as a hobby, it may manifest as your profession also. He's an unknown part of you.

Mansion or attic: God's mansion has many rooms. We visit it to receive gifts. Good things are coming; it may be a talent you should put to use.

Mask: A false front. Are you or is someone else deceiving people?

Mast: Run your beliefs up like a sail for the world to see. God is with you. Put up a sail, God will take you where you need to go.

Mice: To me they mean poverty (poor as a church mouse). Mice were often a focal point of my dreams. I'd be walking and they'd be gathered around my feet. I came to believe I had to learn to accept things the way they were. Shortly thereafter, I dreamed of being dressed in a long gray dress, reminiscent of the pioneer days. I sat down and invited the mice into my lap. I can't recall seeing mice after that.

Milk: A health warning. I once saw myself sitting in the window of a mall store. The photographer was to take my picture. He refused, saying that if I put more milk in my diet, as I had written in the dream book in my lap, I would have better color.

This was a commentary on the state of my health and to look for the truths in my dream journal. I added milk to my diet.

Millionaire: Try to learn something from him. A good money opportunity is at hand. Count your blessings. A part of you, is rich in something. Appreciate it.

Mirror: To see yourself. What do you see? A glimpse of your future? Something may reflect back to you. You're not seeing into the great beyond of the spiritual world. That would be through a window.

Monkey: A description of someone in your life. Is he/she up to monkey business? Are you? It's a part of you.

Monster: Something is wrong. God shocks us this way to wake us up to a fact, gets us to pay attention.

Morning: A fresh beginning.

Mother: If she has passed, she is coming to you for a reason. If she is alive, share the dream with her; it may be a message for her. Depending on how you view your mother, it may be a commentary on yourself. However this character is feeling, it may indicate the same in you.

Mountain: The top is the best place to be. (I once saw myself with some friends and some family on the very top. It was solid rock up there. We could see for miles. I knew it would be okay to stay within this circle of people if I wanted too. I chose not to. Family in another part of the country needed me.)

Mowing: Does the grass need mowing in your dream? Or are you mowing needlessly? Compare this to a needless action in your life.

Moving: A change is needed. This could be a change of attitude, not an actual physical move.

Multiply: A warning of things about to get out of hand. You have time to change it.

Murder: Time to stop something, an attitude, smoking, gambling, lying, etc. (See kill.)

Music: If it is a familiar song, analyze the words with regard to your life. They hold the message. Pay attention to the song running through your mind when you wake up.

Naked: God sees all. Shedding old habits. Better times ahead. Perhaps you fear people knowing the "real" you. We must first learn to love ourselves before we can do good for anyone else.

Negro: If you are Negro, this is a natural state of dreaming. If you are white, you are being asked to see an opposite point of view. Could be one of your shadows, something that's been repressed in your past, good or bad.

Night: A new day is coming.

Noses: Noses prominent in your dreams could be an archetype taken from a myth about fruit trees flowering in the spring. You need a nose to smell them. In my experience I've related prominent noses to be a sign of spring, a new season and birth of new opportunities. "Wake up and smell .." as they say.

Numbers: May be a counting of time till the action of the dream. Three can be a reminder of the trinity. Four can be a need to balance our four needs; family, work, recreation, and religion. Two can also be a balance, as of a scale with two weight trays, a pendulum. Could be an age you need to remember.

Ocean: All water refers to our flow of life. The larger the body of water, the larger part of your life is being encompassed in the message. A pool would be only those people closest to you. The ocean a commentary on world affairs.

Office: Your work life. (I dreamed of papers flying around an office just before the stock market took a huge plunge and Wall Street went crazy. I was not involved with stocks. It was a prediction, a marking of time.)

Officer: An authority figure, an angel's message.

Old: The wisdom available to you. A health warning. An outmoded condition. A past life memory.

Orange: Add more to your diet. Robert J. Hoss, in his book "The Language of Dreams" has a very interesting theory on colors.

Overflow: Something is out of control. Take charge. May mean an abundance. May signify a life's shift, flowing into a new era of life.

Package: A gift, a talent about to be revealed. Use it. Do you feel boxed in?

Pain: A possible problem. Take steps to protect that part of your body. Pain has often let me know I was in another's realm.

Pastor: A spiritual advisor, or you may have a message for one.

Path: Look at the action. We each have a path we should be living and another we <u>are</u> living.

Pavement: Might denote the path you are traveling: spiritual, physical, mental, job, or relationship. Is it smooth?

Pendulum: You are not spending enough time on some important part of your life. Things must balance. Your dreams may be adjusting things for you.

Penis: This is a message about someone in your life. They are living with a huge ego and you must know they are acting from this perspective. (See sex.)

Pink: Love is being heaped upon you or you will shower someone with it yourself.

Plane: The proper use of your talents, the fast track of your career and people in your business world. A young woman told me of a bad recurring dream regarding a plane taking off and getting stuck in some power lines. She gasped with recognition when I replied, "You're not going anywhere, are you?"

Pocketbook: A woman told me she had a recurring dream of being chased by a man who wanted her purse. "Next time you dream this," I said, "see yourself giving the purse to him. Purses are things we women feel we can't be without, but really we can. Is there something in your life that you may be able to give up?" "Yes," she replied, "my son has been after me to sell the family home. I'll do that now." A few days later I received a letter from the son thanking me for interpreting the dream for his mother.

Policeman: A protective angel, an authority, follow the rules, investigate further.

Potato: Adjust your diet. I once saw myself lining up at a door for a progressive dinner. At one door stood a fat lady who served potatoes. At the other door was a thin woman who served rice.

Prize: You are doing a good job.

Purse: See pocketbook.

Questioning: Opening to Spirit. You will receive guidance.

Railroad: The track of your life. I was once sitting beside the track. Going nowhere.

Rain: A cleansing.

Rainbow: Heavenly protection at night and during the day.

Road: Look for signs. You may be in for a big change.

Rock: Solid basis. Be careful of stumbling on your path. You must see it!

Roof: Protection. Or a play on words such as something that goes over the top of your head, as in having missed something. Climb up on it. Can you see further?

Sand: The grains of your chosen life are fragile, futile. Better to travel, study, build your house, upon a rock.

Scales: Justice, balance, an angelic measuring.

School: Obedience and self-discipline are being taught. Apply yourself to things pointed out in your dreams. Where, in life, are you searching for answers?

Search: This is one of those words that will jump out at you in the middle of recording a dream story. For example, "I spent the night searching for...". As you write the word, you will realize this is what the story is about, a search, an uneasiness.

Seat: Throne, perhaps of the master. Sit back, relax.

Sewing: A night, dream-time ministry, building your spiritual garment. Mend a problem.

Sex: Is there a parallel to a life situation? Are you a willing partner? Are you being taken advantage of? Is some situation wearing you out?

Shore: Time to step out of the flow of life and take charge or a need to rest and rejuvenate.

Shower: A cleansing.

Sick: Get a checkup. Stop, take a break, make sure you know what you are feeling and doing.

Sign: Watch for signs. Direction is coming your way.

Sleep: Someone being asleep in your dreams means further study is needed to awaken you to your true spirit.

Snake: A health warning. One woman I dreamed for had many snakes in her dreams. Soon after she was diagnosed with cancer. The sooner the treatment, the better your chance of overcoming it. Also, snakes have been warnings to me when opportunities for trouble would occur that very next day. Wisdom.

Snow: Frozen attitude, useless. It could mean a pure white, spiritual situation.

Soldier: God's army, perhaps regarding a struggle you are involved with. He has come to help you fight your battles. Do you feel you are fighting a battle?

Spider: Beware a web that might catch you. It may be a mythical symbol of the great mother that has built the web to catch what you need. It's coming your way. Congratulations!

Storm: A storm of activity ahead. You are too busy.

Street: The path of life you are on. Will you turn at the next cross street? Take a new direction. Is it busy, commercial? Perhaps too much of your efforts are on one thing. Remember to balance relationships, work, recreation and worship.

String: Tie up loose ends, tell the truth, and do not forget to keep your promises. It may be pointing to a connection between two people or happenings.

Sunlight: A reward, good news. You can see more clearly.

Surprise: A reward lies ahead; a talent will be revealed which you must use.

Swamp: Becoming mired in unclean thoughts.

Swim: Your struggle or race through life.

Table: With white cloth is a meeting with Christ. A place of nourishment.

Teacher: If in a school you have attended, you are still learning lessons from that period in your life. If at your table or a new place, it relates to spiritual /attitudinal lessons. Beware false teachers.

Teeth: Falling out means the illness of a loved one or loosing something vital.

Telephone: Telepathy, the mode of communicating. The message you are receiving in the dream could be from someone living. Call them. Could also mean the message comes from beyond (a higher authority).

Temple or church: A holy place. Holy ground.

Thief: You are stealing from your own potential by your present actions. Turn and ask the thief what he wants. In your dream give it to him. Look for a change in your life. A side of yourself overlooked and now it wants recognition.

Throne: Seat of an important person.

Tiger: (See Lion.)

Tire: On a car symbolizes a part of your life that may need fixing.

Toilet: Going to the bathroom in a dream means your subconscious is working on eliminating a wrong attitude or belief. If, in your dreams, you spend a lot of time in various bathrooms, you need to study life and people more.

Tomato: Add this food to your diet.

Tornado: Beware; a stressful time is ahead. A prediction.

Tower: A higher perspective of things, bringing you greater authority.

Train: A vehicle of life; see vehicle. Ask yourself, what kind of trip are you on?

Treasure: A gift is coming.

Trees: The silent wisdom and protection. The story of life. Spend time near them. Send them love. Communicate with them.

Trouble: A very important message to change something in your life.

Truck: Earth needs, slow spiritual progress.

Tub: Dream concerns only as many people as will fit in this tub. A need to come clean.

Tunnel: Watch action. Are you lost and/or about to come out into the light? Is this a comment on your view of current events, as in tunnel-vision?

Umbrella: You are under the temporary protection of a spirit. Or you may need one today.

Undress: A fear of what the world thinks of you. Perhaps it is time to make public your spiritual beliefs. Find out what you are repressing. To be naked in dreams is because you have no need to hide anything anymore. You are free.

Untie: Let go of the past. Loosen up, you'll feel freer.

Vegetables: Put more of them in your diet.

Vehicles: Airplane = taking off, flying, landing are commentaries on your overall life. Could be a warning. Bus = The community of your commercial endeavors or job. Car = Your personal life. Example: Are you driving it or is someone else telling you what to do? Bike = You alone, usually investigating your level of human progress. Truck = Daily needs, slow progress.

Walking: Do more. You need to exert will power in some situation. It could signify slow steady progress.

Wall: A barrier to what you want. A reminder of the causes and effects of situations. God's universal laws in action; When you bang into a wall and can go no further, turn around. Take a different path. Choose to think differently about something.

War: A struggle in your life. What is consuming you at this time?

Watch: A reminder to be patient. Wait for God's timing. As a play on words, you are being watched to see which direction or what attitude you will choose.

Water: Brown = Deception; Clear = Purity; Ocean = Origins of life; Lake = This lifetime; Pool = Closer sphere of attention (also the method souls use to enter into this life); River = Humanity.

Wave: Difficulties, being tossed, not in control of yourself. Sometimes that's okay.

Wedding: A holy meeting of minds. A blessing. You have entered God's path and will walk in the light. If watching a wedding, you are getting close.

White: Purity and grace; Forgiveness, being in the spirit.

Wind: Cold wind may be death of a plan or signaling the winds of change. A presence of spirit. I once detected living twins by the force of the wind that blew in when I connected with one of them.

Window: See glass and house. An opportunity to see further than before.

Woman: If unknown she may be an angel or Mother Mary. What role does she play in the dream? Most characters are another side of you. She may be an archetype sent to illustrate a story.

Woods: You have the wisdom if you will search for it. As the old saying goes, are you not seeing the forest for the trees? A good play on words, also, might be wood itself. Or, would you really? Cement is stronger.

Work: The dream story is usually job or money related. It may signal a new type of work on the horizon, something you might begin to prepare yourself for. Same old job you used to do? Dreams use what we know to tell us what we don't know.

Worship: Do more. Meditate. Spirit is guiding you through a particular change.

Worm: Unhealthy, whether body or situation. A play on words might be 'Inch by inch, anything's a cinch." Take your time, one day at a time. Low on the scale of things.

Writing: Contact with one's recording angel. 'The writing's on the wall' can be a very clear message. Write!

X-ray: See through to the bone of the situation. Could be a health warning. Making some thing clear. Examine closer!

<u>Yellow:</u> Joy is your essence or in your future.

<u>Young:</u> Some thing in your life is the same age as your attitude or your intellect about which the dream story revolves.

About The Author

Carol Oschmann began dream study to rid herself of stress. Her nightmares were the one thing she could not control. After reading *Edgar Cayce On Dreams*, she adopted the belief that God talks to you in dreams. It confirmed a message she'd heard from a minister when she visited a Baptist church. He said, "I don't know how God talks to you, but He talks to me in my dreams." Her rewards have been many.

Born in upstate New York, the mother of three and grandmother of four, a bookkeeper by trade, she was amazed as her life shifted to that of writer and photographer for a travel magazine, program planner for a T.V. travel program, and dream researcher. Most amazing of all, to her, was her new ability to dream for other people.

Carol graduated from the Haden Institute as a Dream Group Leader. She leads a weekly dream study group in Sun City Center, Florida, has led one in Brandon, Florida, teaches a course in dreams at Sun City Center Community College, writes occasionally for *Dream Network Magazine* and promotes her lecture business. She has given talks on dreams before church groups, senior groups, college alumni groups, Lions Clubs, Rotaries, Community Women's groups, and others. She's talked in churches, college dorms, homes, restaurants and apartment recreation rooms.

Printed in the United States
61229LVS00002B/1-51

9 781929 841455